CW01567023

Contents

National Security Strategy and Strategic Defence and Security Review 2015

A Secure and Prosperous United Kingdom

Presented to Parliament
by the Prime Minister
by Command of Her Majesty

November 2015

Cm 9161

Foreword by the Prime Minister

Our national security depends on our economic security, and vice versa. So the first step in our National Security Strategy is to ensure our economy is, and remains, strong.

Over the last five years we have taken the difficult decisions needed to bring down our deficit and restore our economy to strength. In 2010, the total black hole in the defence budget alone was bigger than the entire defence budget in that year. Now it is back in balance. By sticking to our long-term economic plan, Britain has become the fastest growing major advanced economy in the world for the last two years. Our renewed economic security means we can afford to invest further in our national security.

This is vital at a time when the threats to our country are growing. From the rise of ISIL and greater instability in the Middle East, to the crisis in Ukraine, the threat of cyber attacks and the risk of pandemics, the world is more dangerous and uncertain today than five years ago. So while every government must choose how to spend the money it has available, every penny of which is hard-earned by taxpayers, this Government has taken a clear decision to invest in our security and safeguard our prosperity.

As a result, the United Kingdom is the only major country in the world today which is simultaneously going to meet the NATO target of spending 2% of our GDP on defence and the UN target of spending 0.7% of our GNI on development, while also increasing investment in our security and intelligence agencies and in counter-terrorism.

In ensuring our national security, we will also protect our economic security. As a trading nation with the world's fifth biggest economy, we depend on stability and order in the world. With 5 million British nationals living overseas and our prosperity depending on trade around the world, engagement is not an optional extra, it is fundamental to the success of our nation. We need the sea lanes to stay open and the arteries of global commerce to remain free flowing.

So this document sets out our National Security Strategy for the coming five years, and how we will implement it. It presents a clear vision for a secure and prosperous United Kingdom, with global reach and global influence.

At its heart is an understanding that we cannot choose between conventional defences against state-based threats and the need to counter threats that do not recognise national borders. Today we face both and we must respond to both. So over the course of this Parliament our priorities are to deter state-based threats, tackle terrorism, remain a world leader in cyber security and ensure we have the capability to respond rapidly to crises as they emerge.

To meet these priorities we will continue to harness all the tools of national power available to us, coordinated through the National Security Council, to deliver a 'full-spectrum approach'.

First, over the last five years we have reconfigured Britain's Armed Forces so they are able to deal with modern and evolving threats. Where necessary, we will be ready to use force. We will ensure that our Armed Forces continue to remain world-leading. We will establish two additional Typhoon squadrons and an additional squadron of F35 Lightning combat aircraft to operate from our new aircraft carriers. We will buy nine new Maritime Patrol Aircraft, based in Scotland, to protect our nuclear deterrent, hunt down hostile submarines and enhance our maritime search and rescue. We will create two new Strike Brigades, forces of up to 5,000 personnel fully equipped to deploy rapidly and sustain themselves in the field. By 2025, we will have a highly capable expeditionary force of around 50,000, up from the 30,000 we committed to in 2010. We will double our investment in our Special Forces' equipment. We will maintain our ultimate insurance policy as a nation – our Continuous At Sea Nuclear Deterrent – and replace our four ballistic missile submarines. In the longer term we will also increase the size of the Royal Navy's frigate fleet.

Second, we will do more to ensure our security and intelligence agencies have the resources and information they need to prevent and disrupt plots against this country at every stage. So we will invest an additional £2.5 billion, including employing over 1,900 additional staff and strengthening our network of counter-terrorism experts in the Middle East, North Africa, South Asia and Sub-Saharan Africa. We will also increase our investment in counter-terrorism police and more than double our spending on aviation security around the world.

Third, we will use our outstanding Diplomatic Service to promote our interests and project our influence overseas. We will use our formidable development budget and our soft power to promote British values and to tackle the causes of the security threats we face, not just their consequences. This includes refocusing our aid budget to support fragile and broken states and regions to prevent conflict – and, crucially, to promote the golden thread of conditions that drive prosperity all across the world: the rule of law, good governance and the growth of democracy. These interventions are not just right morally – they are firmly in our national interest. Our substantial aid budget means that Britain not only meets our obligations to the poorest in the world, but can now respond rapidly and decisively to emerging crises overseas which impinge on our security at home – and with this speed and agility of response comes greater influence in the world.

Fourth, Britain's safety and security depends not just on our own efforts, but on working hand in glove with our allies to deal with the common threats that face us all, from terrorism to climate change. When confronted by danger, we are stronger together. So we will play our full part in the alliances which underpin our security and amplify our national power. We will work with our allies in Europe and around the world – as well as seizing opportunities to reach out to emerging powers.

History teaches us that no government can predict the future. We have no way of knowing precisely what course events will take over the next five years: we must expect the unexpected. But we can make sure that we have the versatility and the means to respond to new risks and threats to our security as they arise.

Our Armed Forces, our police and our security and intelligence agencies put their lives on the line every day. Their service is an inspiration to us all and they are the pride of our nation. Through this National Security Strategy and Strategic Defence and Security Review we will back them and use our hard-earned economic strength to support our Armed Forces, and to give those in our police and our security and intelligence agencies who fight terrorism the resources they need to help keep our country safe.

Chapter 1 – Our Vision, Values and Approach

Our vision

1.1   Our vision is for a **secure and prosperous United Kingdom, with global reach and influence**. Everything we do in the UK and around the world is driven by our determination to protect our people and our values, and ensure that our country prospers.

1.2   Economic security goes hand-in-hand with national security. Since 2010 we have restored our economic security to live within our means. We now have one of the fastest growing developed economies. We have chosen to invest in projecting our power, influence and values. We are the only major country in the world to spend both 2% of Gross Domestic Product (GDP) on defence and 0.7% of Gross National Income (GNI) on overseas development. These commitments will increase our security and safeguard our prosperity.

1.3   To underpin our vision, we have an ambitious, forward-looking National Security Strategy:

- We will strengthen our **Armed Forces** and our **security and intelligence agencies** so that they remain world-leading. They project our power globally, and will fight and work alongside our close allies, including the US and France, to deter or defeat our adversaries.

- We will further enhance our position as the world's leading **soft power** promoting our values and interests globally, with our world-class **Diplomatic Service**, commitment to **overseas development**, and institutions such as the BBC World Service and the British Council.

- We will invest more in our current **alliances** including NATO, build stronger relationships with growing powers, and work to bring past adversaries in from the cold.

- We will strengthen our **domestic resilience** and **law enforcement capabilities** against global challenges which increasingly affect our people, communities and businesses.

1.4   In particular, over the next five years our priorities will be to:

- Tackle **terrorism** head-on at home and abroad in a tough and comprehensive way, counter **extremism** and challenge the poisonous ideologies that feed it. We will remain a world leader in **cyber** security. We will **deter** state-based threats. We will respond to **crises** rapidly and effectively and build resilience at home and abroad.

- Help strengthen the **rules-based international order and its institutions**, encouraging reform to enable further participation of growing powers. We will work with our partners to **reduce conflict**, and to promote **stability, good governance and human rights**.

- Promote our **prosperity**, expanding our economic relationship with growing powers such as India and China, helping to build global prosperity, investing in innovation and skills, and supporting UK defence and security exports.

Our values

1.5   The UK has a proud tradition of protecting its people, promoting civil liberties, upholding the rule of law, and building diverse, integrated communities tolerant of different faiths and beliefs. Our democratic and inclusive values are the foundation of our security and prosperity. We will continue to uphold these values against those who are intent on undermining them. We will prevent those who seek to spread extremist ideologies through our communities from doing so.

1.6   Our long-term security and prosperity also depend on a stable international system that reflects our core British values. Democracy, the rule of law, open, accountable governments and institutions, human rights, freedom of speech, property rights and equality of opportunity, including the empowerment of women and girls, are the building blocks of successful societies. They are part of the golden thread of conditions that lead to security and prosperity. Their absence limits opportunities for the individual and drives resentment, political instability and conflict. Ensuring that rights are protected and respected is essential in order to tackle the root causes of conflict and to promote better governance.

Our approach

1.7   In a rapidly changing, globalised world, what happens overseas increasingly directly affects us at home. We need policies and capabilities which enable us to tackle immediate challenges, such as the threat from ISIL; to secure our interests over the longer term; and to respond rapidly to the unexpected. We need allies and partners who support us, and an international system which reflects our values and helps us to protect our interests.

1.8   This strategy sets out our robust and activist approach. We will use the full spectrum of our national power. We will build our defences, resilience and partnerships at home. We will work ever more closely with allies and partners overseas.

1.9   We have organised delivery of our National Security Strategy through three high-level, enduring and mutually supporting **National Security Objectives**. These embody an integrated, whole-of-government approach, supported by greater innovation and efficiency. They are underpinned by new, substantial and targeted investment, made possible by our renewed economic strength.

National Security Objective 1: Protect our people

1.10   National Security Objective 1 is to **protect our people** – at home, in our Overseas Territories and abroad, and to protect our territory, economic security, infrastructure and way of life.

1.11   We have chosen to:

- Meet the NATO pledge to spend 2% of our GDP on defence in every year of this Parliament, guarantee a real increase in the defence budget every year of this Parliament, and create a Joint Security Fund which will grow to £1.5 billion by the end of this Parliament.

- Invest in agile, capable and globally deployable Armed Forces and security and intelligence agencies to protect the UK and project our power globally.

- Exploit the full spectrum of our capabilities and work with our allies to respond robustly to the re-emergence of state-based threats.

- Deter potential adversaries, including through renewal of our nuclear deterrent.

- Prioritise the fight against terrorism, radicalisation and extremism at home and overseas.

- Protect the cross-government counter-terrorism budget.

- Put in place tough and innovative measures, as a world leader in cyber security.

- Strengthen our capabilities to disrupt serious and organised crime and to prosecute criminals.

- Increase our communities' resilience to threats and hazards; and improve the government's crisis management architecture.

National Security Objective 2: Project our global influence

1.12   National Security Objective 2 is to **project our global influence** – reducing the likelihood of threats materialising and affecting the UK, our interests, and those of our allies and partners.

1.13   We have chosen to:

- Spend 0.7% of GNI on Official Development Assistance, which we have enshrined in law, and to make a new commitment to invest at least 50% of the Department for International Development's budget in fragile states and regions.

- Expand our world-leading soft power and our global reach to promote our values and interests, using our diplomats and development assistance, and through institutions such as the BBC World Service and the British Council.

- Invest more in our alliances, build new, stronger partnerships and persuade potential adversaries of the benefits of cooperation, to multiply what we can achieve alone.

- Strengthen the rules-based international order, helping to make both established and newer multilateral institutions fit for the 21st century.

- Build stability overseas, upholding our values and focusing more of our development effort on fragile states and regions.

- Help others overseas to develop their resilience and preparedness, and respond more effectively to the impact of conflict and crises.

National Security Objective 3: Promote our prosperity

1.14   National Security Objective 3 is to **promote our prosperity** – seizing opportunities, working innovatively and supporting UK industry.

1.15   We have chosen to:

- Champion an open and rules-based international trading environment, to build sustainable global prosperity.

- Maximise prosperity opportunities from our defence, security, diplomatic and development activities.

- Work more closely with the private sector and allies to increase our innovation and strengthen its contribution to our national security.

- Support the UK's defence, resilience and security industries to grow, including through exports and through investment in skills.

This document

1.16   The following six chapters set out how we will deliver our vision and strategy, through the National Security Objectives.

1.17   Chapter 2 summarises the UK's unique strengths which enable us to play a strong, positive global role.

1.18   Chapter 3 summarises the changing national security context and the implications for the future. This draws on a range of open and classified material from departments across government, including the National Security Risk Assessment 2015, which we have tested and discussed with external experts and key allies and partners.

1.19   Chapters 4 to 6 set out our detailed strategy, the policies which we will pursue, and the capabilities in which we will invest:

- Chapter 4 on National Security Objective 1 describes how we will protect our people at home, in our Overseas Territories and abroad, and protect our territory, economic security, infrastructure and way of life, using the full spectrum of our national power.

- Chapter 5 on National Security Objective 2 describes how we will project our global influence, reducing the likelihood of threats materialising and affecting us.

- Chapter 6 on National Security Objective 3 describes how we will promote our prosperity, seizing opportunities, working innovatively and supporting UK industry.

1.20   Chapter 7 sets out how we will implement our strategy. This includes new work to increase joint working and efficiency across government, and to ensure that we have the most agile crisis response and early warning mechanisms.

1.21   Annex A summarises the National Security Risk Assessment 2015.

Chapter 2 – The UK: Strong, Influential, Global

The UK: strong, influential, global

2.1   The UK plays a strong, positive global role. We project our power, influence and values to help shape a secure, prosperous future for the UK and to build wider security, stability and prosperity. We have unique strengths that enable us to do this.

2.2   We have one of the fastest-growing developed economies. The World Economic Forum Competitiveness Report assesses the UK to be in the top ten for competitiveness. The UK is the number one destination in Europe for inward investment. We are ranked by the World Bank as the sixth easiest place in the world to do business.

2.3   This allows us to invest in defence and security. The UK's defence budget is the second largest in NATO after the US, and the largest in the EU.

2.4   We have a **strong, diverse and resilient society**. At home, we are strengthening our domestic resilience, giving more power to local communities, investing in infrastructure across the UK, and delivering devolution so that we can focus on how powers are used to better the lives of the people of England, Scotland, Wales and Northern Ireland in a strong United Kingdom.

2.5   Our **Armed Forces** and **security and intelligence agencies** (the Secret Intelligence Service, the Security Service, and the Government Communications Headquarters) are respected around the world for their capability, agility, reach and ability to fight and work alongside our close allies. We took tough decisions to balance the defence budget in 2010, and are now in a position to invest in the highly deployable Armed Forces that we need to guarantee our security. Our **law enforcement organisations** and **judicial system** ensure the security and safety of our people, and are globally respected.

2.6   Our **Diplomatic Service** has a strong, global reputation and is one of the world's most extensive, with our diplomatic network represented in over 85% of the world's countries and missions to all major multilateral organisations. We use it to pursue an active foreign policy that protects our country, our people and our interests, supports the security of our allies, deters adversaries, projects our influence and values, promotes our prosperity, and strengthens the rules-based international order.

2.7   Our position as the world's leading **soft power** gives us international influence. English is the global language, and our time zone allows us to connect with the Americas and Asia in the same working day.

2.8   We are the second largest bilateral aid donor in the world after the US, and the only G7 nation to meet the United Nations/Organisation for Economic Cooperation and Development (OECD) target to spend 0.7% of GNI on **Official Development Assistance**. We have enshrined this commitment in law. Our leadership on international development, including our overseas presence and our research and innovation, enables us to influence a range of partners and multilateral organisations. British non-governmental organisations are highly respected. They promote human rights, the protection of civilians and good governance around the globe.

2.9   Our **media, sports and arts** reach millions around the world. The BBC World Service alone has a global audience of 210 million, and one in every 16 adults around the world watches, listens to, or reads the BBC news. The British Council works in over 110 countries worldwide and is at the forefront of the UK's international networks and soft power.

2.10   The UK is a **global leader in science, technology, medicine, energy, and the creative industries**. We are home to 18 of the world's top 100 universities, and four of the top ten. The UK has significant and growing education links worldwide. More than a quarter of current world leaders have studied in the UK. More than 80% of UK institutions have international partnerships, through which 1.8 million overseas students receive a British education each year. UK companies are leaders in innovation, research and development of new technologies, and high-end goods and services.

2.11   We will use our long-term relationships to develop and maintain the alliances and partnerships that we rely on every day for our security and prosperity.

2.12   Our special relationship with the US remains essential to our national security. It is founded on shared values, and our exceptionally close defence, diplomatic, security and intelligence cooperation. This is amplified through NATO and our Five Eyes intelligence-sharing partnership with the US, Canada, Australia and New Zealand. We are extending and expanding our defence and security relationships with our European partners, notably France through our commitments under the 2010 Lancaster House Treaty, and Germany. We have close relationships with all EU member states, and with allies worldwide such as Japan.

2.13   We have strengthened our security partnerships in the Middle East, especially the Gulf, and in Africa. We are actively promoting closer relationships across the Asia-Pacific region, including with Indonesia, Malaysia, Singapore and the Republic of Korea. We are also building **stronger relationships with growing powers**, including China, India, Brazil and Mexico. The UK was the first major Western country to become a prospective founding member of the Asian Infrastructure Investment Bank, which has received significant support in the region. We continuously look to establish and build productive and open relationships, bringing past adversaries in from the cold while not shying away from addressing areas of divergence.

2.14   We sit **at the heart of the rules-based international order**. The UK is the only nation to be a permanent member of the UN Security Council and in NATO, the EU, the Commonwealth, the G7 and G20, the Organization for Security and Cooperation in Europe, the OECD, the World Trade Organization, the International Monetary Fund and the World Bank.

2.15   We use our membership of these organisations as an instrument to amplify our nation's power and prosperity. In all these organisations, we play a central role in strengthening international norms and promoting our values. We promote good governance, anti-corruption, the rule of law and open societies. We maintain and champion free trade, including through the EU, and we work with growing powers around the world to build a stronger and more resilient global economy.

Chapter 3 – The National Security Context

The changing national security context and future implications

3.1   The world is changing rapidly and fundamentally. We are seeing long-term shifts in the balance of global economic and military power, increasing competition between states, and the emergence of more powerful non-state actors. We are increasingly likely to have to deal with unexpected developments.

3.2   Globalisation and technological advances bring unparalleled opportunities to the UK and to people around the world. But the National Security Risk Assessment 2015 concludes that the threats faced by the UK, including our Overseas Territories and our overseas interests, have increased in scale, diversity and complexity since 2010. A summary of the assessment is at Annex A.

3.3   Four particular challenges are likely to drive UK security priorities for the coming decade. They have both immediate and longer-term implications:

    i. The increasing threat posed by terrorism, extremism and instability.

    ii. The resurgence of state-based threats; and intensifying wider state competition.

    iii. The impact of technology, especially cyber threats; and wider technological developments.

    iv. The erosion of the rules-based international order, making it harder to build consensus and tackle global threats.

3.4   In this dynamic and uncertain context, we will have to work to ensure our security and to exploit opportunities.

Domestic and global security challenges

Terrorism and extremism

3.5   The threat from Islamist terrorist groups to the UK, including to British nationals and interests overseas, has increased. Since 2010, over 60 British nationals have been killed as victims of terrorism overseas, including in the recent attacks in Sousse and Paris. The terrorist threat is fed, supported and sanctioned by extremist ideologies.

3.6   A number of Islamist terrorist groups are active across the Middle East, Africa and South Asia, with increasing reach into Europe. The emergence of ISIL and its brand of violent extremism has significantly increased the threat. ISIL now operates over much of Syria and Iraq, and has affiliates in other countries. ISIL has recruited foreign fighters from most countries in Europe and across the Islamic world. Approximately 800 British nationals have travelled to Syria to take part in the conflict since it began, and many have joined ISIL and other terrorist groups. A large proportion were previously unknown to the police and security agencies. Of those who are known to have travelled about half have returned. Some of these, and many of those who remain in Syria, pose a threat to our security.

3.7   Terrorists have tried to use a wide variety of methods of attack, from unsophisticated knife and gun attacks to more complex plans involving firearms and explosives at multiple locations. Terrorists who are directed or inspired by ISIL pose a direct threat to our security and that of our allies, as demonstrated by recent attacks in Paris as well as in the Middle East and North Africa. Our law enforcement and security and intelligence services have stopped at least seven different attempts to attack the UK in the last 12 months alone. Passenger aircraft remain a primary target for some terrorist groups. Some groups, especially ISIL and Al Qa'ida, will also try to acquire chemical, biological and radiological capabilities.

3.8   Extremist and terrorist groups, in particular ISIL, have exploited the internet and social media to distribute large quantities of often sophisticated online propaganda intended to radicalise and recruit large numbers of people here and in other countries. Terrorist groups also use widely available encrypted online communications to plan attacks. This and other attempts to evade detection mean that it is now much harder for the police and security agencies to spot, investigate and then successfully disrupt terrorist attack planning. It is also difficult to investigate and disrupt terrorist and criminal threats when they originate from states which have poor governance, or which lack credible and effective police and security organisations operating to our human rights standards.

3.9   The significant threat posed by terrorist groups makes it all the more important that we invest to tackle this issue head-on at home and abroad using the full spectrum of our capabilities.

Northern Ireland related terrorism

3.10   There is still a threat from Northern Ireland related terrorism. Violent dissident republicans have sufficient numbers and weapons to pose an enduring threat in Northern Ireland primarily to the police, but also prison officers, members of the Armed Forces, national infrastructure and commercial targets. Violent dissident republicans aspire to target Great Britain, and some groupings remain capable of conducting one-off attacks, but currently consider Northern Ireland to be their main focus.

Impact of instability

3.11   The conflict in Syria and Iraq has shown how crises can trigger and accelerate instability across a region, and the challenges created by state failure or a lack of effective, publicly legitimate and accountable governance. Such challenges include regional instability, large-scale humanitarian need, mass migration and human trafficking, and exploitation of weak governments or ungoverned space by terrorist groups and criminals. Instability overseas also undermines affected countries' prospects for poverty reduction and economic growth.

3.12   Many drivers of instability are likely to persist over the medium to long term, including social inequality and exclusion, demographic changes, rapid and unplanned urbanisation, climate change, and global economic and other shocks. This is why we have chosen to focus more of our development effort on building stability overseas in fragile states.

Migration

3.13   Migration is a global challenge. Instability, extremism and conflict in the Middle East and Africa have displaced millions of people in recent years. Many have sought to travel to Europe, creating a humanitarian challenge and pressures across the EU. Longer-term trends, including increased access to information through mobile technology and social media, are adding to the drivers of migration, as are the activities of criminal networks. As we and others look to deal with the consequences of protracted conflicts, we will need coordinated work with multilateral agencies and countries that are hosting large numbers of refugees, to help improve livelihoods and give displaced people the best possible prospects as close to home as possible. In the light of migration pressures, it will also be vital that we further strengthen our ability to control migration, to offer protection to those who need it, and to ensure that the border, immigration and citizenship system can manage migration overseas, at the UK border and within the UK.

Serious and organised crime

3.14   Serious and organised crime has a direct impact on our security, economy and reputation. It costs the UK at least £24 billion every year. The most significant types include cyber crime, child sexual exploitation and abuse, illegal firearms, organised immigration crime, drug trafficking, economic crime including fraud, money laundering and bribery and corruption. The volume and severity of serious and organised crime threats to the UK are growing, as more services and transactions take place online, internet access expands across Africa and Asia, and technology develops.

3.15   The UK remains the largest centre for cross-border banking, accounting for 17% of the total global value of international bank lending and 41% of global foreign exchange trading. But substantial funds from crime conducted around the world are laundered through London, including in the UK's foreign exchange turnover which is reported as $2.7 trillion in London daily. Closer partnership between government and the financial sector is important in order better to understand the problem and develop innovative solutions.

Global health security

3.16   The risks to health security will continue to grow as the world becomes more physically interconnected through travel. Countries and regions with weak health services or where government ability to respond is poor are especially vulnerable. The Ebola outbreak in West Africa is an example. There has been no onward transmission in the UK, though we exercised local response plans in preparation. But in Sierra Leone, Liberia and Guinea the height of the outbreak led to thousands of deaths and significant disruption to development efforts designed to build stability and a more sustainable future.

3.17   The emergence and spread of microbes with the potential to cause pandemics and the rise of drug resistance, including Antimicrobial Resistance (AMR), are significant concerns. They will require greater and more coordinated action at local, national, regional and global levels. No single nation can act alone on such transnational threats. The UK has taken a leadership role, building international partnerships to tackle AMR and other risks to global health security.

The resurgence of state-based threats

3.18   Competition between states, and the threats they pose to each other, can have a significant impact on our security and our interests. At the extreme, this risks drawing the UK and our allies into military conflict. Regional conflict and instability can also trigger pressure for the evacuation of British nationals. At the less extreme end, uncertainty can affect our prosperity and the prosperity and security of some of our closest allies.

Russian behaviour

3.19   At the NATO summit in Lisbon in 2010, we committed to work with our Allies to build a partnership with Russia. But since then Russia has become more aggressive, authoritarian and nationalist, increasingly defining itself in opposition to the West. The illegal annexation of Crimea in 2014 and continuing support to separatists in eastern Ukraine through the use of deniable, hybrid tactics and media manipulation have shown Russia's willingness to undermine wider international standards of cooperation in order to secure its perceived interests.

3.20   Russia is mid-way through a programme of major investment to modernise and upgrade its military, including its nuclear forces. It has also increased its nuclear exercises and rhetoric, with threats to base nuclear forces in Kaliningrad and Crimea. Its military activity around the territory of our Allies, and close to UK airspace and territorial waters, is designed to test our responses. Russia's behaviour will continue to be hard to predict, and, though highly unlikely, we cannot rule out the possibility that it may feel tempted to act aggressively against NATO Allies.

3.21   Our commitment to collective defence and security through NATO remains as strong as ever. The 2014 Wales Summit, under UK leadership, delivered an effective and united response to Russian behaviour. NATO's commitments include the Allies' defence investment pledge and the Readiness Action Plan, which respond to the challenges posed by Russia and their strategic implications, as well as to risks and threats to the south of Europe. With NATO Allies we have made the Very High Readiness Joint Task Force a reality and our contributions to the NATO Air Policing Mission in the Baltics will remain important to deter threats. At UK urging, the EU has imposed sanctions designed to change Russian behaviour.

3.22   Russia is one of the five permanent members of the UN Security Council, and notwithstanding our differences, we will seek ways of cooperating and engaging with Russia on a range of global security issues, such as the threat from ISIL.

Wider state competition

3.23   Foreign intelligence agencies continue to engage in hostile activity against the UK and our interests, and against many of our close allies. This includes human, technical and cyber operations at home and overseas to compromise the UK Government, diplomatic missions, government-held information and Critical National Infrastructure (CNI); attempts to influence government policy covertly for their benefit; and operations to steal commercial secrets and disrupt the private sector. Compromise or damage from these attacks may not be immediately visible.

3.24   More generally, wider state competition can be a risk to stability. In the Middle East and North Africa, regional powers have been pursuing competing security interests, driven by growing military and economic capabilities. Both South Asia and South East Asia continue to grow in economic importance and political significance, but this has come with increased tensions, exacerbated by unresolved historical disputes. North Korea is the only state to test a nuclear weapon in the 21st century, and its continued pursuit of nuclear weapons and ballistic missiles is a serious concern.

The role of technology

Cyber

3.25   The UK increasingly relies on networked technology in all areas of society, business and government, and this has brought significant benefits. There is inherent resilience in the internet's decentralised nature. But we are vulnerable to attacks on parts of networks that are essential for the day-to-day running of the country and our economy.

3.26   The range of cyber actors threatening the UK has grown. The threat is increasingly asymmetric and global. Reliable, consistent cyber defence typically requires advanced skills and substantial investment. But growing numbers of states, with state-level resources, are developing advanced capabilities which are potentially deployable in conflicts, including against CNI and government institutions. And non-state actors, including terrorists and cyber criminals can use easily available cyber tools and technology for destructive purposes.

3.27   New forms of communication empower individuals and groups to communicate rapidly. But encrypted communications, often provided by global companies operating outside the UK, will continue to be used by terrorists and organised crime groups. The relationship between individual privacy and national security is increasingly challenging, and increasingly important to get right. For security reasons, Western states will want access – within a narrow set of tightly prescribed circumstances – to travel, financial and communications data held by other states and by the private sector. Conversely, the proliferation of cyber capabilities will make it ever harder to protect the information and well-being of private individuals, corporations and states.

Wider technological developments

3.28   Advances in medical technology, genetic engineering, biotechnology, materials science, big data and robotics hold huge potential for our security and prosperity. For example, new detection and screening technologies can better protect our borders, CNI and crowded places. This technology will be more effective because it can be deployed routinely by the private sector in support of national security.

3.29   But such technology will also become available to more state and non-state actors, including terrorists, organised crime groups and cyber criminals. This could reduce Western states' technological advantage as controls on access to knowledge and materials become harder to maintain.

3.30   The UK is reliant on access to space for our security, our economy, disaster management and military capabilities. But near-Earth orbits are becoming increasingly congested and competitive, with more countries and private actors pursuing space programmes.

3.31   Innovative and competitive UK defence and security industries play a major part in addressing the threats we face. Innovation in the products and services that they provide helps to maintain our advantage over adversaries. Ensuring that they are globally competitive helps to sustain the skills and capabilities that we need.

The rules-based international order

3.32   The rules-based international order is founded on relationships between states and through international institutions, with shared rules and agreements on behaviour. It has enabled economic integration and security cooperation to expand, to the benefit of people around the world. It has done much to encourage predictable behaviour by states and the non-violent management of disputes, and has led states to develop political and economic arrangements at home which favour open markets, the rule of law, participation and accountability. The UK has consistently championed this framework.

3.33   The context is changing, driven by developments such as the growing role of non-state actors, the impact of technology and longer-term shifts of economic wealth to the south and east of the world. The Chinese economy is expected to become larger than that of the US in the 2020s, while other emerging markets, in particular India and Brazil, have the potential to grow markedly in power and influence. While the US, Japan and Europe will remain global economic powers, they face a growing imperative to improve their economic dynamism and competitiveness if they are to stay at the cutting edge of the global economy – which our reform efforts with the EU are intended to help address.

3.34   Such changes create new challenges and opportunities. The rules-based international order has always relied for its effectiveness and legitimacy on the active participation and contribution of all states, in particular major states, and on the ability of institutions and relationships to adapt to reflect new opportunities and challenges. It will therefore be important to reflect the contribution of growing powers. We will continue to work with partners to adapt the rules-based international order to meet new challenges.

3.35   The rules-based international order also relies on enforcement of standards and laws covering a wide range of activities and behaviours, from the Geneva Conventions to the UN Convention on the Law of the Sea. There have been successes, in particular the work by the E3+3 (the UK, France, Germany, the US, China and Russia) and the EU to conclude the Joint Comprehensive Plan of Action with Iran so that it meets its obligations to ensure its nuclear programme is exclusively peaceful. Some powerful states and non-state actors, however, are increasingly ignoring international norms that they believe run contrary to their interests, or favour the West. Russia's illegal annexation of Crimea, Assad's use of chemical weapons, and the challenges around non-state actors' compliance with international humanitarian law are examples of this.

Continuing risks

3.36   There are a number of other risks which remain important and need to be addressed.

Civil emergencies

3.37   Severe flooding during 2013/14 affected more than 13,000 properties in the UK. The last five years have also seen outbreaks of public disorder (in 2011), and the threat of substantial nationwide disruption brought about by industrial action. We need to be prepared to respond quickly and effectively to frequent and unpredictable emergencies, both locally and where necessary nationally.

Major natural disasters overseas

3.38   Major natural disasters overseas can put at risk the safety and security of British nationals, our CNI and the supply chains on which we rely, such as energy, food and technology. Our response often includes a humanitarian element. For example, after the Nepal earthquake in 2015, the UK provided a humanitarian and reconstruction aid package as well as assistance on the ground.

Energy security

3.39   Global energy security can be affected by regional disputes, instability, terrorism and cyber threats, and more positively by technological developments.

3.40   Our investments in nuclear, shale, renewable and other innovative technologies will increasingly generate new sources of energy for the UK. But oil and gas production from the UK continental shelf will gradually decline and our reliance on imported hydrocarbons is likely to grow over the next few decades. Currently, around 40% of the oil we use is imported, and projections suggest that this could increase to 73% by 2030. Further measures to protect and diversify sources of supply will become increasingly important, including the new Southern Corridor pipeline, US liquid natural gas (LNG) exports, further supplies of Australian LNG, and increased supply from Norway and North Africa. Working through international energy organisations and expanding their membership is an important way of mitigating future supply risks and managing growing demand effectively.

The global economy

3.41   Advanced economies have made a slow though meaningful recovery from the global economic crisis. But progress has been uneven and vulnerabilities remain, particularly in the euro area and Japan. Recent downward revisions of long-term growth potential in both advanced and emerging economies are a concern, and should spur action to deliver structural reforms that can drive long-run productivity growth. Despite considerable progress, China still faces significant challenges in delivering the necessary reforms for a more sustainable growth model. Commodity exporters face difficult adjustments amid declining prices. The growing level of corporate debt in emerging markets increases risks, especially where it leads to greater foreign currency exposure. Russia's actions in Ukraine and continuing instability in the Middle East, North and West Africa illustrate the scope for political disputes adversely to affect global markets and regional growth prospects.

Climate change and resource scarcity

3.42   By 2030, the world could face demands for 50% more food and energy and 30% more water, while their availability becomes threatened by climate change. The Middle East and North Africa region will be particularly at risk, given existing high levels of water stress and high rates of population growth. Sub-Saharan Africa may suffer from climate change impacts on crop production in particular. Rising sea levels threaten coastal cities and small islands. More frequent extreme weather events are likely to disrupt populations, agriculture and supply chains, making political instability, conflict and migration more likely.

3.43   In contrast to the West's ageing populations, almost 50% of the world's population is under the age of 24, the vast majority in developing countries. This presents opportunities in terms of potential for driving economic growth. But risks include under-employment, an increase in existing resource stresses, greater instability and migration pressures.

Chapter 4 – Protect Our People

Overview

4.1   National Security Objective 1 is to **protect our people** – at home, in our Overseas Territories and abroad, and to protect our territory, economic security, infrastructure and way of life.

4.2   This chapter sets out how the Government will use the full spectrum of our capabilities to do this. In particular, we will invest in our **Armed Forces** and **security and intelligence agencies**; deter potential adversaries, including with our **nuclear deterrent**; combat **extremism and terrorism** at home and overseas; put in place tough and innovative **cyber security** measures; strengthen our ability to disrupt **serious and organised crime**; and increase our **resilience** against threats and hazards.

4.3   This is an integrated, cross-government effort, at home and overseas. For example, our **domestic** work is led by the Home Office, but also involves a wide range of other government and law enforcement agencies. Our **security and intelligence agencies** work closely together, and with law enforcement, military, industry and international partners, to protect our national security. Our **diplomatic** work led by the Foreign and Commonwealth Office (FCO) builds effective, long-term partnerships overseas, which enable us better to disrupt threats to the UK and tackle them at source.

A. Protecting the UK, Overseas Territories and British nationals overseas

4.4   The Government's most important duty is the defence of the UK and Overseas Territories, and protection of our people and sovereignty.

4.5   We will tackle all threats to the UK, our people and our interests. The UK will remain resilient to, and a hostile environment for, those who intend us harm, whether they are state-based or non-state actors such as terrorists and criminals, and we will coordinate all levers of national power so that the sum of our efforts is greater than the constituent parts.

Deterrence

4.6   Defence and protection start with deterrence, which has long been, and remains, at the heart of the UK's national security policy. Deterrence means that any potential aggressors know that any benefits they may seek to gain by attacking the UK will be outweighed by the consequences for them.

4.7   We will use the full spectrum of our capabilities – armed force including, ultimately, our nuclear deterrent, diplomacy, law enforcement, economic policy, offensive cyber, and covert means – to deter adversaries and to deny them opportunities to attack us. We will use these to ensure that there are consequences for those who threaten our security. We will build our resilience to reduce our vulnerabilities.

4.8   We will uphold and strengthen the rules-based international order to ensure that those who transgress international law and agreed standards of behaviour are held to account, including through the use of economic sanctions. If our adversaries reject or operate outside these bounds, we will act decisively, and use our influence, including through our membership of international organisations, to persuade others to take a similarly tough stance.

4.9   We will use our world-class security and intelligence agencies, technological advantage, diplomats and law enforcement to enable us to stay ahead of our adversaries and to frustrate their goals. We will increase funding for the security and intelligence agencies to enable £2.5 billion of additional investment in staff and capabilities. More than half of this investment will be on counter-terrorism. **We will recruit and train over 1,900 additional security and intelligence staff across the agencies to respond to, and deter those behind, the increasing international terrorist, cyber and other global threats.**

4.10   We will treat a cyber attack on the UK as seriously as we would do an equivalent conventional attack, and we will defend ourselves as necessary.

4.11   We are strengthening our Armed Forces so that they remain the most capable in Europe, are able to project our power globally, and fight and work alongside our close allies to deter or defeat our adversaries. We remain ready and willing to use armed force when necessary to protect our national interests.

4.12   The collective defence and cooperative security provided by our membership of NATO further enhances the credibility of our deterrence. We will also work with our key allies across the world to multiply the effects of our own determined approach and increase our collective security. **In NATO, we will lead a renewed focus on deterrence to address current and future threats**, and to ensure that our potential adversaries are in no doubt about the range of responses they should expect to any aggressive action on their part.

Our sovereignty

4.13   We will use all of our capabilities to defend our sovereignty and territorial integrity, and our Armed Forces are ready to use force when required. We are also protected through our membership of NATO. Article 5 of the North Atlantic Treaty states that an armed attack against one state shall be considered an attack on all.

4.14   There is currently no immediate direct military threat to the UK mainland. But, with increasing frequency, our responses are tested by aircraft, including Russian aircraft, near our airspace, and maritime activity near our territorial waters. The Royal Air Force protects our airspace and is ready at all times to intercept rogue aircraft. The Royal Navy protects our waters, and deters terrorist and criminal activity. Our NATO Allies provide us with early warning of approaching ships and aircraft, or deal with them before they reach our territory or airspace, as we do for our Allies. Our investment in Maritime Patrol Aircraft will significantly improve our ability to maintain our maritime security.

4.15   In 2011 we established the UK National Maritime Information Centre to coordinate information about our maritime security, nationally and with international partners. **We will enhance joint working between law enforcement agencies and the Royal Navy to increase patrolling in our territorial waters.** We will also improve aerial surveillance operations and information sharing across government.

4.16   The UK has been under constant threat from ballistic missiles since the Second World War. But states outside the Euro-Atlantic area and non-state actors are now acquiring ballistic missile technology. The threat faced by the UK, our Overseas Territories and our military bases has evolved. We will continue to commit significant funds to the NATO Ballistic Missile Defence (BMD) network, as well as supporting research and development initiatives and multinational engagement through the UK's Missile Defence Centre. We will invest in a ground-based BMD radar, which will enhance the coverage and effectiveness of the NATO BMD system. We will also investigate further the potential of the Type 45 Destroyers to operate in a BMD role.

Our Overseas Territories

4.17   Our 14 Overseas Territories retain a constitutional link with the UK. Our relationship, while rooted in centuries of shared history, is a modern one, based on mutual benefits and responsibilities. We take our responsibilities seriously and will continue to support these communities and their right to safety, security and self-determination.

4.18   We will continue to work closely with the Falkland Islanders to defend their right to self-determination, which is enshrined in the Charter of the UN. They face an unjustified claim of ownership from Argentina. We judge the risk of a military attack to be low, but we will retain a deterrence posture, with sufficient military forces in the region, including Royal Navy warships, Army units and RAF Typhoon aircraft. We will invest up to £300 million over the next 10 years to enhance operational communications, renew the existing air defence system and upgrade infrastructure.

4.19   Some of our Overseas Territories face threats from transnational crimes such as illegal migration, narcotics smuggling, money laundering and illegal fishing. In the Caribbean in particular, we are working with our Overseas Territories to improve security and law enforcement. There are also risks from climate change, natural disasters and hostile foreign activity. We will continue to build our Overseas Territories' resilience, crisis preparedness and response.

4.20   We have increased the manning of the Royal Navy Gibraltar Squadron and improved our ability to monitor Gibraltar's territorial waters. We will continue to challenge all incursions. In Cyprus, two Army infantry battalions contribute to the security of the Sovereign Base Areas and we are increasing manning levels at RAF Akrotiri airfield to provide better support to ongoing operations against ISIL and in the wider region. This will also enable us to evacuate British nationals or to conduct hostage rescue missions more quickly.

Combating hostile foreign intelligence activity

4.21   The UK is a target for hostile foreign intelligence activity because we are an advanced economy, have a sophisticated military, and wield international influence as a member of NATO, the EU and the G7 and as a permanent member of the UN Security Council. The threat, by its very nature, is covert. Our defences must be robust, protecting our most valuable assets and national security investments.

4.22   We will increase departmental accountability for decisions on protective security across government, including personnel, physical and cyber security. We will improve information sharing across government, CNI and key industrial partners.

Our borders

4.23   The UK is a global hub. Over 200 million people and £700 billion of international trade cross our borders each year, and numbers are increasing. The UK is not part of the EU's Schengen open borders agreement, and so we have been able to set our own approach to the migration crisis caused by instability in the Middle East and Africa by taking refugees directly.

4.24   Legitimate passengers and goods must be able to travel without hindrance. But our borders are also a critical line of defence at which we can and do identify and disrupt threats to our security, including from terrorism and serious and organised crime.

4.25   We have significantly strengthened border security. We created the Border Force in 2012 and the National Crime Agency's (NCA) Border Policing Command in 2013. We have established five Joint Border Intelligence Units to target developing threats.

4.26   We will strengthen our ability to detect the movements of people and goods such as illegal firearms that present a threat, through detection technology and better data on land, sea and air passengers and cargo, and through intelligence and targeting. We will modernise and introduce more automation to enable us to deploy our border officials where they are needed most, including an enhanced presence at our sea ports.

4.27   Although radiological and nuclear threats are unlikely to occur, we will continue to counter them. We will work with international partners to invest in new technology, to ensure that the radiological and nuclear detection systems at the UK border remain among the best in the world.

Consular assistance and protecting British nationals overseas

4.28   Five million British nationals live overseas, and British nationals make an estimated 60 million visits abroad each year. The FCO's Travel Advice website is used by 27 million people a year, helping them to make informed decisions before they travel. Travel operators and companies which employ British nationals overseas should also have emergency plans. The FCO answers almost a million consular enquiries from British nationals each year, and provides consular assistance when needed. In 2014, this included more than 16,500 cases.

4.29   We respond rapidly to crises overseas, such as terrorist attacks, natural disasters and outbreaks of conflict or public disorder, in order to protect British nationals and British interests. If needed, we help people to leave a country, and in extreme situations we organise evacuations. Our strong relationships overseas enable us to secure cooperation and assistance from host governments in times of crisis.

4.30   We have strengthened our ability to respond rapidly through our surge capacity of crisis-trained FCO Rapid Deployment Teams. We will train and exercise more of our staff in crisis response and build expertise. We will maintain our specialist kidnap negotiation and hostage rescue capabilities. We have a long-held and clear policy on ransoms: we do not pay ransoms to terrorists.

4.31   We will continue to collaborate with our allies to support the development of other countries' crisis response, and to help to build crisis management and protective security capabilities in countries where British interests could be affected.

B. Our Armed Forces

4.32   The essential role of our Armed Forces is to defend the UK so that we can live in peace.

4.33   Since 2010, we have restored our economic security and balanced the defence budget. **We will continue to meet the NATO target to invest 2% of GDP on defence**, which will allow us to:

- Increase the defence budget in real terms every year of this Parliament.

- Deliver our commitment to maintain the size of the regular Armed Forces and to not reduce the Army to below 82,000, and increase the Royal Navy and Royal Air Force by a total of 700 personnel.

- Deliver our commitment to increase the equipment budget by at least 1% in real terms and continue to meet the NATO target to spend 20% of the defence budget on researching, developing and procuring new equipment.

- Establish a new Joint Security Fund, from which the Ministry of Defence (MOD) will draw.

We will allow the MOD to invest efficiency savings into the Armed Forces.

4.34   We have reformed the MOD and Armed Forces, including by improving our procurement process, to ensure that we can maximise investment in the front line. **We will spend £178 billion over the next decade on equipment and equipment support.** We will also take steps to increase the productivity of the Armed Forces, enhancing their fighting power still further.

4.35   The MOD also contributes to our economic security, supports our industry including through innovation and exports, and continues to invest 1.2% of the defence budget on science and technology.

4.36   Over the last five years, we have learned lessons from operations in Libya, Afghanistan, the Middle East, Sierra Leone and elsewhere. We will build on the adaptable approach we took in 2010, and ensure that the Armed Forces remain flexible and agile over the next 10 years.

Defence policy

4.37   To support the delivery of this strategy, our defence policy sets the Armed Forces eight missions. Routinely, they will:

- **Defend and contribute to the security and resilience of the UK and Overseas Territories.** This includes deterring attacks; defending our airspace, territorial waters and cyber space; countering terrorism at home and abroad; supporting the UK civil authorities in strengthening resilience; and protecting our people overseas.

- **Provide the nuclear deterrent.** This mission is set out in Section C of this chapter.

Joint Force 2025

JOINT – Joint Headquarters, Forces and Enablers

Special Forces Squadrons

Special Reconnaissance and Support

Secure IT and Communications Systems

Skynet 5 Space Operations Centre

Defence Intelligence

Joint Cyber Group

Defence Medical and Dental Services

(including 3 Field Hospitals)

MARITIME – Delivery of the Deterrent and a Maritime Task Group from:

 4 x SSBN (Nuclear Deterrent)

 7 x SSN (Hunter Killer Submarines)

 2 x Aircraft Carriers

 19 x Destroyers and Frigates

 Up to 6 x Patrol Vessels

 12 x Mine Hunters / 3 x Survey Vessels / 1 x Ice Patrol Ship

 3 Commando Brigade / 2 x Landing Platform Dock / 3 x Landing Ship Dock

 6 x Fleet Tankers / 3 x Fleet Solid Support Ships

 4 x Merlin Mk2 Squadrons / 2 x Wildcat Squadrons

LAND – A war-fighting Division from:

 2 x Armoured Infantry Brigades

 2 x Strike Brigades

 16 Air Assault Brigade

 6 x Infantry Brigades (also conduct overseas engagement and UK resilience tasks)

 77 Brigade (counter hybrid warfare)

 1 ISR Brigade (Intelligence, Surveillance and Reconnaissance)

 4 x Apache Squadrons / 4 x Wildcat Squadrons / 3 x Watchkeeper Batteries

 2 x Puma Squadrons / 3 x Chinook Squadrons / 2 x Merlin Mk4 Squadrons

 Enabling capabilities (Artillery, Engineers and Logistics)

AIR – An Air Group from:

 >20 x Protector

 9 x P8 Maritime Patrol Aircraft

 3 x Rivet Joint / 6 x E-3D Sentry / 8 x Shadow

 2 x F35 Lightning Squadrons

 7 x Typhoon Squadrons

 6 x Force Protection Wings

 14 x Voyager

 8 x C17

 22 x A400M Atlas / 14 x C130J Hercules

STRATEGIC BASE – Ministry of Defence & Permanent Operating Bases

Strategic Headquarters

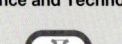

Global defence network

Science and Technology

Research and Development

Whole Force Approach

Military, civilian, industry collaboration

Equipment support

Logistics

- **Contribute to improved understanding of the world through strategic intelligence and the global defence network.** This includes close and enduring work with our allies and partners during peace and conflict.

- **Reinforce international security and the collective capacity of our allies, partners and multilateral institutions.** This includes work to help shape the international security environment, and to strengthen the rules-based international order including through conflict prevention, capacity building and counter proliferation. This is covered in Chapter 5.

The Armed Forces will also contribute to the Government's response to crises by being prepared to:

- **Support humanitarian assistance and disaster response, and conduct rescue missions.**

- **Conduct strike operations.**

- **Conduct operations to restore peace and stability.**

- **Conduct major combat operations if required, including under NATO Article 5.**

Joint Force 2025

4.38   We will ensure that the Armed Forces are able to tackle a wider range of more sophisticated potential adversaries. They will project power, be able to deploy more quickly and for longer periods, and make best use of new technology. We will maintain our military advantage and extend it into new areas, including cyber and space. **We will develop a new Joint Force 2025** to do this, building on Future Force 2020.

4.39   Joint Force 2025 will increase our Armed Forces' ability to work with the rest of government and internationally. **We will enhance the Armed Forces' capability to work alongside the security and intelligence agencies to disrupt threats in the most challenging operating environments worldwide.** While our Armed Forces can and will whenever necessary deploy on their own, we would normally expect them to deploy with allies such as the US and France; through NATO; or as part of a broader coalition. The Armed Forces also undertake permanent tasks, including territorial defence, delivering the nuclear deterrent, and assisting the UK civil authorities' resilience and ability to respond to terrorism.

4.40   We will be able to deploy a larger force more quickly. By 2025, this highly capable expeditionary force of around 50,000 (compared with around 30,000 planned in Future Force 2020) will include:

- A maritime task group centred on a Queen Elizabeth Class aircraft carrier with F35 Lightning combat aircraft.

- A land division with three brigades including a new Strike Force.

- An air group of combat, transport and surveillance aircraft.

- A Special Forces task group.

4.41   When the Armed Forces are not deployed at this scale, they will be able to undertake a large number of smaller operations simultaneously. These might include:

- A medium-scale operation, often drawing mostly on just one Service, such as our current counter-ISIL mission in Iraq.

- Multiple additional operations, ranging from specialist missions such as counter-terrorism or counter-piracy, through to broader, more complex operations such as the military support to tackle Ebola in Sierra Leone or the enduring naval presence in the Gulf.

- A wide range of defence engagement activities, such as training teams and mentoring.

4.42   Joint Force 2025 will be underpinned by significant policy changes: in personnel policy to ensure that the Armed Forces can recruit and retain the people they need in a competitive employment market; a stronger international focus in defence; and a defence innovation initiative to ensure that we remain in step with our closest allies and ahead of our adversaries. **We will develop proposals to ensure that the Armed Forces can operate effectively overseas and are not subject to unjustified legal claims that undermine their ability to do their job.**

Joint Forces Command

4.43   The MOD will build on the success of the Joint Forces Command, which was set up in 2012 to champion the critical capabilities needed by all three Services and to support the command of operations through the Permanent Joint Headquarters.

4.44   Joint Forces Command will lead the MOD's work to improve its understanding of our security environment, using new information technology and greater analytical power to exploit big data, social media and both open source and classified material. We will maintain our satellite communications and invest in cyber and space capabilities. We will protect our networks, and attack those of our adversaries if necessary. We will strengthen our command and control systems, enabling them to work more easily with our NATO Allies, especially the US and France, and across government. We will improve our deployed logistical and medical capabilities by facilitating greater access to experts in the UK.

Special Forces

4.45   Our Special Forces undertake the most dangerous and difficult missions to keep us safe. We will more than double our current planned investment in Special Forces equipment to enhance their ability to operate and strike globally in the most hostile environments on their own or with our closest allies, and in particular to enhance their counter-terrorism capabilities.

4.46   We will buy advanced communications equipment and weapons, and ensure that our Special Forces can operate covertly around the world. They will have the information they need, including through our investment in advanced high-altitude surveillance aircraft. We will upgrade our helicopters and transport aircraft so that they can deploy further and faster.

The Royal Navy

4.47   The Royal Navy delivers our nuclear deterrent, projects our maritime power and provides world-class amphibious forces. As part of Joint Force 2025, we will have:

- Two new Queen Elizabeth Class aircraft carriers, the largest warships ever built for the Royal Navy. These will enter service from 2018, transforming the Royal Navy's ability to project our influence overseas. They will form the core of our maritime task group, with one available at all times. We will increase the number of F35 Lightning aircraft we are buying in the early 2020s to ensure that we make best use of this world-leading capability, and we will buy three new logistic ships to support the fleet, in addition to the four tankers that will enter service from 2016.

- Type 45 destroyers, Type 23 frigates, Astute Class submarines and Mine Countermeasure Vessels. We will maintain one of the most capable anti-submarine fleets in the world with the introduction of eight advanced Type 26 Global Combat Ships, which will start to replace our current Type 23 frigates in their anti-submarine role. We will maintain our fleet of 19 frigates and destroyers. We will also launch a concept study and then design and build a new class of lighter, flexible general purpose frigates so that by the 2030s we can further increase the total number of frigates and destroyers. These general purpose frigates are also likely to offer increased export potential. We will buy two further new Offshore Patrol Vessels, increasing the Royal Navy's ability to defend UK interests at home and abroad.

- Royal Marines of 3 Commando Brigade who are trained and equipped to provide specialist amphibious and Arctic warfare capabilities. We will enhance a Queen Elizabeth Class aircraft carrier to support this amphibious capability.

The Army

4.48   The Army delivers a modern, capable and sophisticated force able to fight independently or alongside our allies, train international partners and contribute to the UK's resilience. As part of Joint Force 2025, we will have:

- A war-fighting division optimised for high intensity combat operations. The division will draw on two armoured infantry brigades and two new Strike Brigades to deliver a deployed division of three brigades. We will establish these two Strike Brigades to be able to deploy rapidly over long distances using the new Ajax armoured vehicles and new mechanised infantry vehicles. They will double the number of brigades ready for operations. With these, and 16 Air Assault Brigade's very high readiness forces, we will improve our ability to respond to all likely threats.

- Upgraded Apache attack and RAF Chinook support helicopters, and Warrior armoured fighting vehicles. We will extend the life of our Challenger 2 main battle tanks.

- Two innovative brigades comprising a mix of Regulars and specialist capabilities from the Reserves able to contribute to our strategic communications, tackle hybrid warfare and deliver better battlefield intelligence.

- A number of infantry battalions reconfigured to provide an increased contribution to countering terrorism and building stability overseas. They will conduct defence engagement and capacity building, providing training, assistance, advice and mentoring to our partners.

The Royal Air Force

4.49   The Royal Air Force defends our airspace, projects our air power globally and provides vital intelligence to support operations including counter-terrorism. We will continue to operate Tornado combat aircraft until they are replaced by Typhoon. As part of Joint Force 2025, we will have:

- Typhoon and F35 Lightning aircraft, which will ensure that the Royal Air Force can continue to deal with evolving threats. We will establish an additional F35 Lightning squadron and two additional Typhoon squadrons. We will invest further in Typhoon's capabilities, including ground attack and a new Active Electronically Scanned Array radar to ensure that we can continue to operate it until at least 2040. We will maintain our plan to buy 138 F35 Lightning aircraft over the life of the programme.

- Complex weapons, including Stormshadow and Brimstone missiles, which offer unrivalled precision. We will continue to invest further in new precision weapons to sustain our battle-winning capabilities.

- More than 20 new Protector armed remotely piloted aircraft, more than doubling the number of the Reaper aircraft which they replace.

- Upgraded aircraft to gather intelligence and detect and track targets, both on the ground and in the air. Sentinel will be extended in service into the next decade; Shadow until at least 2030; and Sentry and Rivet Joint until 2035.

- Nine new Boeing P8 Maritime Patrol Aircraft to increase further the protection of our nuclear deterrent and our new aircraft carriers. These aircraft will be based in Scotland and will also have an overland surveillance capability.

- A recapitalised air transport fleet to enable our Armed Forces to intervene globally at speed. By 2016, we will have 14 Voyager air-to-air refuelling aircraft. Our 22 new A400M Atlas heavy-lift aircraft will enhance our global reach, alongside our eight C17 aircraft. We will upgrade and extend the life of our C130J aircraft, allowing them to support a range of operations until 2030.

- A recapitalised Command Support Air Transport fleet to replace the current aircraft as they reach the end of their life. This will increase their operational utility and ensure we are able to continue to transport the Royal Family and senior Ministers cost-effectively. We will also adapt one of our existing Voyager aircraft so that, as well as its primary air tanking role, it can transport senior Ministers securely, delivering better value for money than the current use of charter aircraft. The aircraft would also be available to the Royal Family.

4.50   We will invest in the next generation of combat aircraft technology, in partnership with our defence aerospace industry and our closest allies. We are working with the US to build and support the F35 Lightning. **We will work with France to develop our Unmanned Combat Air System programme, and collaborate on complex weapons.**

Our people

4.51   Our Armed Forces rely on the skills, commitment and professionalism of our people. We place heavy demands on them. Recruiting, training and retaining the right mix of capable and motivated Service personnel is essential to deliver success on operations. **We are committed to maintaining the size of the regular Armed Forces and to not reduce the regular Army below 82,000.**

4.52   We will continue to develop the 'Whole Force' approach, ensuring that we use both Regular and Reserve members of the Armed Forces, and that we use MOD civil servants and contractors to support the front line, deploying forward when required. We will make it easier for people to move between the different elements of the 'Whole Force' over their career, and we will work collaboratively with industry to make skills available across organisational boundaries when and where needed.

4.53   We will ensure that a career in the Armed Forces can be balanced better with family life. **We will make the changes necessary to enable our Armed Forces to work flexibly, reflecting the realities of modern life. We will make a new accommodation offer to help more Service personnel live in private accommodation and meet their aspirations for home ownership.**

4.54   We will introduce a new pay model for those serving in the Armed Forces. It will be simpler and better targeted. We will also begin to phase out commitment bonuses, which have not proved effective, and reinvest the savings into the Armed Forces. There will be no reductions in Armed Forces numbers.

4.55   **We will develop a new Armed Forces offer for new joiners, which better meets the expectations of future recruits and targets resources on the people we need most.**

4.56   The **Reserves** are an essential part of our Armed Forces. They allow us to access skills and expertise found in the civilian world. Reserve personnel help to link the Armed Forces to society, and employers benefit significantly from the transferable skills that Reserve personnel bring to their businesses. **We will continue to grow our Reserves to 35,000**, with increased investment in training and equipment and improved pay and conditions.

4.57   We are committed to achieving an inclusive working environment, and to building Armed Forces that are diverse and fully representative of UK society. This will be the work of many years but, as a step towards this goal, by 2020 the Armed Forces will be recruiting at least 10% Black, Asian and Minority Ethnic personnel and at least 15% women. The review of women in combat has concluded that in principle, there is no reason why they should not be able to undertake the full range of combat roles. We are conducting a study of the physiological impacts of these roles and based on this work, we will announce a final decision on women undertaking the full range of combat roles in 2016.

4.58   Our commitment to the Armed Forces is set out in the **Armed Forces Covenant**, which we enshrined in law in the Armed Forces Act 2011. Its key principles are that those who serve in the Armed Forces, whether Regular or Reserve, those who have served in the past, and their families, should face no disadvantage; and that special treatment is appropriate in some cases, especially for those who have given the most, such as the wounded, injured and sick. Every local authority in Great Britain and over 700 corporate employers have committed to the Covenant.

4.59   We are delivering a comprehensive programme to ensure that the Armed Forces receive the overall support that they deserve. We have committed over £450 million of banking fines to support Armed Forces charities, and, working with the devolved administrations, continue to develop policies in education, healthcare, tax and housing to cater for the unique needs of Service life. **We will launch the first comprehensive families strategy for the Armed Forces**, doing more on spousal employment, healthcare and children's education. We will further improve access to financial services. And we will strengthen the Armed Forces Covenant to support our veterans in finding civilian employment.

4.60   Defence **civil servants** make an important contribution to our national security, including through their roles on operations and in delivering some of the largest and most complex equipment and infrastructure projects found anywhere in government.

4.61   We will continue to reform the MOD to make it leaner and more efficient, outsourcing key functions where the private sector can deliver better, and investing in skills for the roles we retain. **We will reduce the number of civilians employed by the MOD by almost 30%, to 41,000, by the end of this Parliament.**

Defence estate

4.62   The defence estate includes the land, accommodation and training facilities that support our Service personnel and are essential to the delivery of military capability.

The MOD's current basing footprint does not meet the needs of our modern Armed Forces. We will make the MOD's estate better suited, while reducing it and making it more affordable. **We will invest in key defence sites, and reduce the built estate by 30%, releasing public sector land for 55,000 new homes to support wider prosperity objectives.**

C. The nuclear deterrent

The role of the nuclear deterrent

4.63   The UK's independent nuclear deterrent will remain essential to our security today, and for as long as the global security situation demands. It has existed for over 60 years to deter the most extreme threats to our national security and way of life, helping to guarantee our security, and that of our allies. Since 1969, the Royal Navy has delivered the nuclear deterrent under Operation Relentless, with at least one of four nuclear-armed submarines on patrol at all times.

4.64   Other states continue to have nuclear arsenals and there is a continuing risk of further proliferation of nuclear weapons. There is a risk that states might use their nuclear capability to threaten us, try to constrain our decision making in a crisis or sponsor nuclear terrorism. Recent changes in the international security context remind us that we cannot relax our guard. We cannot rule out further shifts which would put us, or our NATO Allies, under grave threat.

4.65   The Vanguard Class of nuclear-armed submarines will begin to leave service by the early 2030s. The time it will take to design, develop and manufacture its replacement means that the decisions that we take now will affect our security into the 2050s. It would be irresponsible to assume that the UK will not in the foreseeable future be confronted with the kinds of extreme threat to our security or way of life which nuclear weapons seek to deter. We judge that a minimum, credible, independent nuclear deterrent, based on Continuous At Sea Deterrence and assigned to the defence of NATO, remains vital to our national security. We will therefore make the necessary investment to sustain our Continuous At Sea Deterrence.

The UK's minimum, assured, credible nuclear deterrent

4.66   We are committed to maintaining the minimum amount of destructive power needed to deter any aggressor. This requires us to ensure that our deterrent is not vulnerable to pre-emptive action by potential adversaries. Our assessment, after considering the alternatives, remains that four submarines are needed, in order to give assurance that at least one will always be at sea, undetected, on a Continuous At Sea Deterrent patrol. Submarines on patrol will continue to carry 40 nuclear warheads and no more than eight operational missiles. We will retain no more than 120 operationally available warheads and, by the mid-2020s, we will reduce the overall nuclear weapon stockpile to no more than 180 warheads, meeting the commitments set out in the 2010 SDSR.

4.67   We will continue to keep our nuclear posture under constant review in the light of the international security environment and the actions of potential adversaries.

UK nuclear weapons policy

4.68   Only the Prime Minister can authorise the launch of nuclear weapons, which ensures that political control is maintained at all times. We would use our nuclear weapons only in extreme circumstances of self-defence, including the defence of our NATO Allies. While our resolve and capability to do so if necessary is beyond doubt, we will remain deliberately ambiguous about precisely when, how and at what scale we would contemplate their use, in order not to simplify the calculations of any potential aggressor.

4.69   The UK will not use, or threaten to use, nuclear weapons against any Non-Nuclear Weapons State party to the Treaty on the Non-Proliferation of Nuclear Weapons (NPT). This assurance does not apply to any state in material breach of those non-proliferation obligations. While there is currently no direct threat to the UK or its vital interests from states developing weapons of mass destruction, such as chemical and biological capabilities, we reserve the right to review this assurance if the future threat, development or proliferation of these weapons make it necessary.

Working with NATO, the US and France

4.70   Nuclear deterrence is an important part of NATO's overall strategy. Since 1962, the UK has declared our nuclear capability to the defence of the Alliance, thereby contributing to the ultimate guarantee of collective Euro-Atlantic security.

4.71   The UK works closely with the US and France on nuclear matters, including nuclear policy. UK and US nuclear defence cooperation is underpinned by the recently renewed 1958 Mutual Defence Agreement and the 1963 Polaris Sales Agreement. Among other things, these allow the UK to reduce costs by procuring Trident missiles and other components from the US while maintaining full operational independence. We collaborate with France under the 2010 Teutates Treaty to develop the technologies associated with the safe and effective maintenance of our respective nuclear stockpiles.

Replacement warheads

4.72   Work continues to determine the optimum life of the UK's existing nuclear warhead stockpile and the range of replacement options. A replacement warhead is not required until at least the late 2030s, possibly later. Given lead times, however, a decision on replacing the warhead may be required in this Parliament or early in the next. In the meantime, we continue to invest significantly in the Atomic Weapons Establishment to maintain the facilities and skills necessary to assure the safety and security of the current stockpile, and to sustain the ability to develop a replacement warhead when we need to do so.

The Successor submarine programme

4.73   **We will replace the Vanguard Class of nuclear-armed submarines with a new class of four submarines, currently known as Successor.** This is a national endeavour, and is one of the largest government investment programmes, equivalent in scale to Crossrail or High Speed 2.

4.74   In 2011 we started the design phase. Since then, the MOD has worked with its main industrial partners – BAE Systems, Rolls-Royce and Babcock – to deliver the submarine programme. Improvements are required to deliver this national endeavour, drawing on the experience of major projects in government and the private sector in the UK and beyond. We will create a world-class, enduring submarine enterprise. This will require sustained long-term effort, but we are committed to doing so and will be taking a number of important steps in this Parliament.

4.75   **Working with industry, we will confirm and implement the organisational, managerial and contractual changes needed to deliver the Successor programme.** To do so, we will:

- Establish a new team in the MOD headed by an experienced, commercial specialist to act as the single sponsor for all aspects of the defence nuclear enterprise, from procurement to disposal, with responsibility for submarines, nuclear warheads, skills, related infrastructure and day-to-day nuclear policy.

- Strengthen our arrangements for the procurement and in-service support of nuclear submarines, establishing a new delivery body with the authority and freedom to recruit and retain the best people to manage the submarine enterprise.

- Intensify efforts, with our industrial partners, to improve performance, including through sustained investment in skills and infrastructure.

- Put in place new industrial and commercial arrangements between government and industry, moving away from a traditional single 'Main Gate' approach, which is not appropriate for a programme of this scale and complexity, to a staged investment programme.

- Further invest more than £600 million in the design phase, including buying essential long-lead items for the fourth submarine. This will take the total cost of the design phase to £3.9 billion.

- Finalise investment proposals to begin the next phase, focused on risk reduction and demonstration, in 2016.

4.76   This will be a 20-year acquisition programme. Our latest estimate is that manufacturing the four Successor submarines is likely to cost a total of £31 billion (including inflation over the lifetime of the programme), with the first submarine entering service in the early 2030s. We will also set a contingency of £10 billion. The revised cost and schedule reflect the greater understanding we now have about the detailed design of the submarines and their manufacture.

4.77   We are committed to delivering this vital but demanding and complex programme. **We will hold a debate in Parliament on the principle of Continuous At Sea Deterrence and our plans for Successor, and will continue to provide annual reports to Parliament.**

Nuclear proliferation and our commitments to international treaties

4.78   We will continue to build trust and confidence between Nuclear and Non-Nuclear Weapon States, and to take tangible steps towards a safer and more stable world, where countries with nuclear weapons feel able to relinquish them. We have reduced our own nuclear forces by over half from their Cold War peak in the late 1970s. Of the recognised Nuclear Weapons States, we possess only approximately 1% of the total global stockpile of nuclear weapons. Our submarines on patrol are at several days' notice to fire and, since 1994, we do not target our missiles at any state.

4.79   As a responsible Nuclear Weapons State we are committed to the long-term goal of a world without nuclear weapons and we recognise our obligations under all three of the pillars of the NPT. We will work with our international partners to tackle proliferation and to make progress on multilateral disarmament. The UK plays a leading role on disarmament verification with the US and Norway. We will continue to press for key steps towards multilateral disarmament, including the entry into force of the Comprehensive Nuclear Test Ban Treaty, and successful negotiations on a Fissile Material Cut-Off Treaty in the Conference on Disarmament.

D. Combating extremism and terrorism

Extremism and international terrorism

4.80   The UK faces a significant threat from both extremism and terrorism.

4.81   We define extremism as vocal or active opposition to our fundamental values, including democracy, the rule of law, individual liberty, and mutual respect and tolerance of different faiths and beliefs. We also regard calls for the death of members of our Armed Forces as extremist.

4.82   Extremism, even where it does not break the law, divides communities and weakens the social fabric of our country. It often discriminates on the basis of faith, gender and race; and it normalises intolerance, hatred and bigotry. Extremist ideas are often also used to try to justify terrorism. Terrorist organisations and propagandists for terror routinely draw on extreme ideologies.

4.83   The UK's current terrorism threat level is Severe, meaning that a terrorist attack on the UK mainland is highly likely, and since 2010, over 60 British nationals have been killed by terrorists abroad. The volume and scale of the threat in the UK and overseas is increasing, and its nature has changed, notably with the emergence of ISIL and its affiliates in addition to other Islamist terrorist groups such as Al Qa'ida. ISIL is radicalising large numbers of people, often using social media, and is seeking to inspire or direct them to conduct terrorist attacks in the West or to travel to Syria and Iraq.

4.84   As the terrorist threat has changed, we have updated and strengthened our response, building on our counter-terrorism strategy known as CONTEST, which we published in 2011. For example, the Counter-Terrorism and Security Act 2015 included a wide range of measures to deal with threats linked to Syria and Iraq. **We will update CONTEST in 2016 through a new National Security Council (NSC) committee on Counter-Terrorism, chaired by the Prime Minister.**

Preventing people from being radicalised

4.85   We will continue to take action to stop people being radicalised and drawn into extremism and terrorism. **We will implement our new Counter-Extremism Strategy**, published in October 2015. We will counter extremist ideologies; build partnerships with all those opposed to extremism; disrupt extremists; and build more cohesive communities. We will defend and promote the values which unite us: we are proud of these values, and they are the basis for our diverse, multi-racial, multi-faith society.

4.86   Extremism is a global challenge. We will campaign for a more robust and effective international response to refute extremist ideology and propaganda, including through the UN Secretary General's Action Plan on Preventing Violent Extremism. We will build partners' capacity and willingness to take action against extremist groups and to tackle the root causes of extremism, as well as its violent manifestations, particularly in countries where the UK has a direct interest.

4.87   We will continue to implement the statutory duty which we introduced in the Counter-Terrorism and Security Act in 2015, which means that all local authorities, schools, colleges, universities, NHS and Foundation Trusts, police, probation services and prisons have a specific legal responsibility to prevent radicalisation. We will also expand our work to intervene with people who are at risk of radicalisation and to stop them before they begin to engage in any terrorist-related activity.

Pursuing the terrorists

4.88   We will continue to take action to investigate, disrupt and wherever possible convict terrorists. We will continue to give law enforcement, security and intelligence agencies and our Armed Forces the capabilities to deal with attack planning in the UK and overseas, and in particular the means to deal with terrorists' growing use of encrypted online communications and digital media.

4.89   **We will increase the resources for counter-terrorism police and the security and intelligence agencies to pursue terrorists.** In the police, we will provide more investigators, more police based overseas, and capabilities to investigate terrorist activity online and to process large amounts of digital media quickly and effectively. In the security and intelligence agencies, we will establish a new counter-terrorism operation centre with increased numbers of analysts and investigators, increase our global counter-terrorism reach, and upgrade our counter-terrorism technology, including technical intelligence collection and digital forensic capability.

4.90   The ability to acquire intelligence and evidence from electronic communications, subject to strict safeguards, is and will remain vital to the effective work of law enforcement and the security and intelligence agencies. **In 2016, we will legislate to consolidate the investigatory powers that the public authorities require, with robust oversight, transparency and safeguards, and to ensure that the law keeps pace as communications technology advances.** This legislation will build on the recommendations of three independent reviews published in the past year. It will update powers on the interception of communications, communications data and equipment, and will create the right to appeal to a higher court in the UK against decisions made by the Investigatory Powers Tribunal. It will overhaul and strengthen the existing scrutiny and oversight regime by establishing a new Investigatory Powers Commissioner, and give the public clarity about how the Government's investigatory powers and capabilities are used. Through legislation such as the Justice and Security Act 2013, we have a robust legal and policy framework ensuring that the authorities' actions are effective, necessary and proportionate. We will continue to maximise security, while implementing strict safeguards to ensure that privacy is protected.

4.91   We will ensure that terrorists who are convicted in the UK are then effectively monitored and managed in prisons. We will make further resources available to the police and to the National Offender Management Service for this purpose.

4.92   Terrorism thrives in unstable states and amid civil wars. We need to be able to find and track terrorists in these hostile environments. Where they pose an imminent threat to the UK, British interests abroad or to our allies, and there is no way to bring them to justice, we will act decisively. **We will provide significant new investment to enhance our Special Forces' Intelligence, Surveillance and Reconnaissance and global strike capability.**

Protecting ourselves from attacks

4.93   We will continue to invest in capabilities to protect ourselves against terrorist attack. We will invest in the protection of our transport systems, notably aviation, our borders, our CNI, and crowded places. We will continue to invest in systems which give us data in advance about people intending to come to this country, so that they can be checked against our records.

4.94   Aviation security requires good intelligence, and robust security arrangements. Airlines, airports and governments all have a role to play. **We will more than double our spending on aviation security around the world**, with more British experts able to act overseas, working side by side with host nations in the most vulnerable locations. We will invest in developing new technologies to keep pace with evolving risks, and to help airports and airlines to screen out threats.

4.95   We will work with other countries where British nationals are most at risk from terrorism, to build protective security capacity and capability in order to reduce the risk to the countries themselves and to British interests. Wherever possible, we will collaborate with our allies in this work. **We will create a bigger and more capable global security and intelligence network to protect British citizens at home and abroad, and to work with our partners.**

Preparing to respond to terrorist attacks

4.96   Our ability to respond to terrorist actions relies on our broader crisis response. We have taken significant action to enhance our ability to respond to attacks, hazards and accidents. We will continue to train police, fire and ambulance personnel to work together when responding to major incidents, including chemical, biological, radiological or nuclear incidents before specialists arrive.

4.97   We continue to enhance the ability of emergency services specialists to deal with multiple, major terrorist attacks and to save lives under high-risk conditions. We regularly exercise at local and national levels our response to a potential terrorist firearms attack or siege. We will monitor the threat, and learn lessons from our exercises and from international terrorist atrocities to inform and strengthen our procedures. We will invest in enhanced rapid reaction intelligence collection capabilities to respond to marauding attackers or hostage incidents in the UK.

4.98   Our Armed Forces are also ready to provide support, if needed, in the event of a terrorist attack. We have 10,000 military personnel available on standby to assist the civil authorities for significant terrorist incidents at short notice, supported by a wide range of niche military experts and equipment, such as bomb disposal specialists.

International collaboration

4.99   We will continue to work with close allies and partners including NATO and the EU, and with vital partners, such as Saudi Arabia, in the Middle East. In particular, we will work closely with France under the 2010 Lancaster House Treaty to enhance further our shared efforts to prevent and protect ourselves from terrorism, and pursue those responsible for attacks.

4.100   We will collaborate with a range of countries where we have identified a high threat and a high risk to British interests. **We will increase our network of counter-terrorism and counter-extremism experts in the Middle East, North Africa, South Asia and Sub-Saharan Africa**, with staff from across government and the police. This network will build the capacity and encourage the willingness of governments in these regions to tackle terrorism and extremism, reinforcing our wider efforts to tackle conflict and build stability. We will share UK insights and expertise in counter-extremism, counter-radicalisation and communications; exchange information and conduct joint operations to tackle specific threats; train law enforcement officers, prosecutors and judges; help other countries to develop effective protective security standards and enforce them; and share the latest techniques in responding effectively to attacks.

Northern Ireland related terrorism

4.101 The threat level from Northern Ireland related terrorism remains Severe in Northern Ireland and Moderate in Great Britain. The threat is from violent dissident republican groupings which retain lethal intent and capability, and whose targets are primarily the police but also prison officers and members of the Armed Forces. We continue to work to reduce this enduring threat. We provided £231 million of additional security funding to the Police Service of Northern Ireland from 2011 to 2015.

4.102 The Government will maintain our investment in capabilities to keep the people of Northern Ireland safe. The Security Service, the Police Service of Northern Ireland and the police in the Republic of Ireland will continue to work together to investigate and disrupt the evolving threat from violent dissident republicans.

E. Cyber

4.103 British businesses and government, including the security and intelligence agencies, have made the UK a world leader in cyber security.

4.104 In 2011 we published the UK's first National Cyber Security Strategy. Since then we have invested £860 million in new technology and capabilities. We established the Centre for Cyber Assessment and the UK's Computer Emergency Response Team (CERT-UK). We have built a close partnership between government, the private sector and academia, sharing research, driving innovation and supporting our growing digital economy. We share our specialist knowledge with allies, and cyber defence is part of NATO's core task of collective defence, which could lead to an Article 5 response to a cyber attack threatening national security, stability and prosperity.

4.105 **We will invest £1.9 billion over the next five years in protecting the UK from cyber attack and developing our sovereign capabilities in cyber space. In 2016 we will publish a second five-year National Cyber Security Strategy, and we will launch a further five-year National Cyber Security Programme.** These will ensure that we have in place all the necessary components to defend the UK from cyber attack. These include capabilities that allow us to understand and tackle the most advanced threats, law enforcement capabilities to deal with cyber crime, support for businesses particularly in the UK's CNI, and the skills and innovation needed for the long term.

Detection, defence and response

4.106 The volume and complexity of cyber attacks against the UK are rising sharply, as are the costs to business. It is becoming easier to put together an advanced attack because of software readily available on the black market.

4.107 **We will invest in capabilities to detect and analyse cyber threats, pre-empt attacks and track down those responsible.** Primarily based in the Government Communications Headquarters (GCHQ), these capabilities will enable us to match the pace of technological change. We will continue to share knowledge with British industry and with allies.

4.108 **We will develop a series of measures to actively defend ourselves against cyber attacks**. These national capabilities, developed and operated by the private sector, will reinforce the UK's reputation for being one of the safest places in the world to do business.

4.109 We will improve our national ability to respond quickly and effectively to cyber attack. **We will create a new National Cyber Centre to lead this response.** Operating under GCHQ leadership, it will manage our future operational response to cyber incidents, ensuring that we can protect the UK against serious attacks and minimise their impact. We will pursue a robust policy of challenging those who attempt to use cyber capabilities to cause the UK harm.

4.110 We all have a role to play in protecting computers, networks and data. We will improve the way government protects its data by applying appropriately high standards of cyber security to government systems, introducing stronger defences for our systems and maintaining public confidence in our online government services. **We will build a new secure, cross-government network to improve joint working on sensitive cyber issues.**

4.111 **We will help companies and the public to do more to protect their own data from cyber threats**, providing specialist information to those who need it. This will include simplifying private sector access to government cyber security advice, and our new National Cyber Centre will form a single point of contact for companies seeking advice. Our approach to protecting CNI is described later in this chapter.

4.112 The Government will ensure that our Armed Forces have strong cyber defences, and that in the event of a significant cyber incident in the UK, they are ready to provide assistance. We will provide the Armed Forces with advanced offensive cyber capabilities, drawing on the National Offensive Cyber Programme which is run in partnership between the MOD and GCHQ. We will continue to help NATO and other allies to protect their networks using our intelligence and technical insights, and we will use our advanced capabilities to enable the success of coalition operations.

Cyber crime

4.113 Since 2010, we have invested in new law enforcement capabilities, including establishing the National Cyber Crime Unit within the NCA. We have improved the skills of law enforcement officers and our understanding of cyber crime. **We will reinforce law enforcement's specialist capabilities**, making it more difficult for cyber criminals to operate from within the UK. **We will work with industry to strengthen our ability to disrupt cyber crime**, sharing more information on the threat.

4.114 Most of the cyber criminals threatening the UK are based overseas, often exploiting the anonymity of the internet or the absence of effective cyber law enforcement in their host countries. We will disrupt the activities of cyber criminals overseas through prosecution and other means. **We will create a new intelligence unit dedicated to tackling the criminal use of the 'dark web'.**

International response

4.115 The UK has led the international debate about what responsible behaviour looks like and how international law applies. Through the London Cyber Process, we have challenged partners to do more to build an open, secure and resilient cyber space, and to work together to tackle criminality.

4.116 We will continue to build an international consensus around the acceptable use of cyber space, increasing the political risk for states which attack the UK or our allies.

We will build the capacity of our partners to tackle the cyber threat at source, maximising the likelihood that cyber attacks will fail and be traced back to the point of origin.

F. Serious and organised crime

4.117 Serious and organised crime affects the lives of ordinary people, businesses and government.

4.118 In 2013 we launched the Serious and Organised Crime Strategy and established the National Crime Agency (NCA). We introduced new legislation through the Serious Crime Act 2015 and the Modern Slavery Act 2015. We have strengthened our international partnerships to take joint action and to help build local law enforcement and criminal justice capacity.

4.119 Our aim remains to reduce substantially the level of serious and organised crime affecting the UK and our interests.

4.120 We will focus our resources on tackling the criminal gangs which pose the greatest threats; on reducing the most significant vulnerabilities, including those created as criminals seek to exploit technological developments; and on improving intelligence and analysis.

4.121 We will strengthen digital intelligence and investigative capabilities at national, regional and local levels, and at our borders. We will continue to develop an effective, consistent and coordinated regional law enforcement network. We will continue to take a comprehensive approach to tackling serious and organised crime and terrorism, maximising the effectiveness and efficiency of our overall effort and spend in tackling both these threats.

4.122 While national security is a reserved matter, crime and policing are devolved for Scotland and Northern Ireland. The UK Government will continue to work closely with the devolved administrations to tackle serious and organised crime. We will also ensure that the NCA and other government organisations continue to develop national capabilities.

Illegal firearms

4.123 **We will continue our work to choke off the supply and availability of illegal firearms to prevent their use by criminal or terrorist groups in the UK.** We will ensure that we have the right intelligence, detection, and enforcement capabilities and policies, internationally, at the UK border, and within the country. We will press for stronger EU-wide action to tackle the illegal possession and trafficking of firearms, to set more stringent standards for deactivation, and to encourage greater information sharing.

Illicit finance, corruption and fraud

4.124 **We will introduce new measures to make the UK a more hostile place for those seeking to move, hide or use the proceeds of crime and corruption or to evade sanctions.** We will enhance our cooperation with the private sector, harnessing the capabilities and expertise in the banking, legal and accountancy sectors. We will build on the work of the Joint Money Laundering Intelligence Taskforce and publish a comprehensive action plan to tackle money laundering and to address the gaps in the UK's current response. As set out in Chapter 5, the UK will host a global anti-corruption summit in 2016.

4.125 We will enhance our ability to protect the public, businesses and the public sector from fraud and cyber crime. We will continue to improve the current national reporting mechanism, Action Fraud. We will also establish new relationships and joint capabilities with the private sector, harnessing their analytical capabilities, supported by effective information and intelligence sharing arrangements.

Modern slavery and immigration crime

4.126 **We will ensure that we have the right capabilities in the UK and overseas, and a comprehensive action plan, to better identify, disrupt and dismantle the criminal networks involved in modern slavery and immigration crime.** These networks include those involved in facilitating illegal migration to the UK, and in the wider abuse of our immigration system.

Child sexual exploitation

4.127 **We will strengthen our approach to tackling online child sexual exploitation and abuse.** We will reduce its prevalence by protecting children to reduce vulnerability, making environments safer both online and in our communities, identifying and bringing more offenders to justice and exploring new ways of deterring potential offenders and tackling offending behaviours. We will also do more to reduce the harm caused when sexual abuse does taken place by supporting victims, helping them to recover and avoid repeat victimisation, and by reducing criminals' reoffending. In all of this, we will continue to work with industry and secure a coordinated global response to online child sexual exploitation through the WePROTECT initiative.

G. Crisis response and resilience

4.128 The UK's resilience depends on all of us – the emergency services, local and central government, businesses, communities and individual members of the public.

4.129 The Government continues to build partnerships and draw on lessons learned. Over the last five years we have brought greater senior oversight of the UK's security and resilience through an NSC sub-committee on Threats, Hazards, Resilience and Contingencies. We have increased our use of military expertise to support our planning.

4.130 We have strengthened cooperation between the police, security and intelligence services and Armed Forces, between the UK Government and the devolved administrations, and between the UK and international partners. We have established a global reputation for hosting major international events safely and securely, including the London 2012 Olympic and Paralympic Games. We are putting this experience to good use, providing advice and services to future hosts of major events, and creating opportunities for UK companies.

4.131 We have learned lessons from major incidents overseas. We have detailed, robust and comprehensive plans in place and the necessary capacity to deal with infectious diseases, including pandemic influenza and respiratory diseases. As a result of the Ebola outbreak in West Africa, we have further refined the measures we take to safeguard public health. **We will publish a national bio-security strategy in 2016**, addressing the threat of natural disease outbreaks, as well as the less likely threat of biological materials being used in a deliberate attack.

4.132 We will expand and deepen the Government's partnership with the private and voluntary sectors, and with communities and individuals, as it is on these relationships that the resilience of the UK ultimately rests. We will concentrate in particular on improving the resilience of our CNI, our energy security and our resilience to major flooding.

Resilience arrangements in Scotland, Wales and Northern Ireland

4.133 The handling of the response to an emergency that occurs in, or affects, Scotland, Wales or Northern Ireland will depend on whether or not the emergency relates to a devolved or reserved matter. In areas of reserved responsibility, the UK Government's lead department will lead the response, working closely with the devolved administration.

4.134 Each of the devolved administrations has tried and tested arrangements in place to coordinate the responses to aspects of emergencies for which they are responsible. There are arrangements in place for local cross-border coordination between responders, where required. In the most challenging emergencies, especially where they have consequences for the whole of the UK, there are established arrangements for linking the UK Government's emergency coordination structures with those of the devolved administrations, to ensure that we have a coordinated response.

Critical National Infrastructure (CNI)

4.135 Our CNI includes all the essential mechanisms which keep the country functioning, ranging from the core functions of government, through to ensuring the availability of food and water, fuel and reliable communications.

4.136 Large parts of our infrastructure are in the private sector. The Government will work with infrastructure owners and operators to mitigate risks to our CNI from malicious attack and from natural hazards. **We will make sure that the Government has the right regulatory framework to ensure that our CNI is resilient to future threats.**

4.137 We will work with owners and operators to strengthen the cyber security of our infrastructure. We will establish a cyber training centre and test lab to support the development of more secure technology for use in our CNI, and we will drive up standards of CNI security.

4.138 Essential services must be able to carry on running in the unlikely event of a widespread power cut. **We will enhance the UK's resilience to power disruptions**, and we will work with critical sectors to ensure that new measures are tested and reliable.

4.139 Responsibilities for infrastructure policing are shared across a number of organisations with different levels of capability and capacity, and different arrangements for funding, oversight, regulation and legislation. **We intend to integrate infrastructure policing further and we will review options to do this.**

Energy security

4.140 The UK will meet future energy needs from both domestic production and imports from overseas. We aim to ensure that consumers have secure, sustainable and affordable access to the energy they need, managing the risks posed by regional instability, climate change, natural events and rising global demand.

4.141 We will tackle energy security challenges robustly. We have balanced the need for a competitive energy market with government action to ensure a diverse supply of energy for consumers. As part of this we are modernising the UK's energy infrastructure, including by attracting inward investors, with appropriate assessment of any national security risks, and mitigation. This approach has resulted in the recent investment by China into the new Hinkley Point C nuclear power station, supporting our longer term energy security.

4.142 We will take further action to protect the UK from the market uncertainties caused by instability in the Middle East and Russia's actions in Europe's eastern neighbourhood. We will promote investment in renewable, shale and other innovative technologies to increase domestic production, reflecting devolved arrangements where relevant, and support UK energy companies to win business overseas. We will work with the EU to shape the single energy market, helping to reduce the EU's energy dependence on Russia. We will lead efforts to evolve international energy governance, reducing market distortions and better integrating major non-OECD consumers into decision making.

Flooding

4.143 We have learned valuable lessons from our experience in responding to serious flooding over the past five years, particularly the winter floods in 2013/14. We are investing in building and maintaining flood defences in England.

4.144 It is not possible to prevent all flooding, and so maintaining and improving flood response capability is crucial in order to protect lives. We will put in place a consistent approach to managing flood risk, verifying this through local and national exercises and targeting resources to where they will have the greatest benefit. We will also build the strongest possible partnerships with local authorities, utility companies and businesses.

Partnerships and local responses

4.145 We recognise that the response to, and recovery from, an emergency is carried out first and foremost at the local level. As well as the police, fire and rescue and health services, a wide range of organisations could be involved. These include local government, voluntary service organisations, businesses, community groups and individuals. We will therefore continue to develop and improve coordination between local and national levels of response.

4.146 We will also support local organisations' ability to adapt to changing risks, through:

- Embedding work already under way to ensure that emergency responders work effectively together at the scene of major incidents.

- Helping organisations involved in planning for response to share and apply learning from exercises and real-life events.

- Providing advice, support and infrastructure (including the successful 'ResilienceDirect' digital information-sharing platform) to enable them to fulfil their statutory responsibilities to work together to assess risk, plan and communicate.

4.147 We will develop a new set of resilience standards. We will draw on the expertise of the Voluntary Sector Civil Protection Forum to support planning, response and recovery at the local level. We will also continue to support the Prince of Wales' Business Emergency Recovery Group, a business-led initiative that helps businesses and communities prepare for, respond to and recover from crises.

4.148 The Armed Forces support civil authorities when needed in times of emergency. This ranges from providing specialist teams after aircraft crashes, to ensuring continuity of essential services during industrial action. We have helped local responders understand the support that the Armed Forces can provide and how to access it quickly. We have integrated military experts and planners more closely into local planning and emergency response, and conducted more preparatory exercises at local and regional levels.

4.149 To improve our response further, we will place military planners in key government departments to give the military a wider and more formal role in supporting national resilience contingency planning. We will regularly review the National Risk Register and associated contingency plans to identify areas where the Armed Forces can contribute more. This is in addition to the 10,000 military personnel available on standby to assist the civil authorities for significant terrorist incidents.

Space

4.150 Satellites support our everyday lives, and the space industry is growing rapidly, contributing directly to our prosperity. But space is increasingly congested, with risks of collisions and from other nations' space activities. **We will publish a National Space Policy with a Ministerial committee to coordinate action on both prosperity and security.**

4.151 We will establish a process to mitigate the impact of threats and hazards in space, working with industry to share information and expertise. We will work with international partners to improve space weather forecasts and develop our capacity to respond to events such as major disruptive solar flares.

4.152 We will work with international partners, including the Five Eyes Combined Space Operations initiative and the EU, to contribute to global efforts to ensure a safe and secure space environment. We will enhance our space surveillance capabilities, enabling us to assess space threats, risks and events, both natural and man-made.

4.153 Satellite signals are central to daily life, from smartphones and financial transactions to complex military equipment. Although the US Global Positioning System will remain the standard for secure navigation systems, we will enhance the resilience of military users and key domestic resilience responders using new technologies incorporating the European Galileo system. We will support UK industry to become leaders in developing Galileo-related technology.

4.154 The global reach of our Armed Forces depends on resilient satellite communications, currently provided by the Skynet 5 constellation. In collaboration with our allies, we will pursue innovative technologies and make our global communications operations resilient to current and emerging threats, including jamming and cyber attack.

Chapter 5 – Project Our Global Influence

Overview

5.1   National Security Objective 2 is to **project our global influence** – reducing the likelihood of threats materialising and affecting the UK, our interests, and those of our allies and partners.

5.2   This chapter sets out how the Government will use our **global influence** to protect and promote our interests and values, supporting our security and prosperity. We will use our diplomats, development assistance, Armed Forces, security and intelligence agencies, law enforcement and soft power. We will invest more in our relationships with our traditional **allies and partners** and build stronger partnerships around the world, to multiply what we can achieve alone. We will work with our allies and partners to strengthen, adapt and extend the **rules-based international order** and its institutions, enabling further participation of growing powers. We will be more ambitious in **tackling conflict and building stability overseas**, and we will help others to develop their resilience and preparedness, including for the global challenges of climate and health security.

A. Global influence

5.3   Our influence, across foreign, defence and security policy, development, business and academia, and through our cultural and people-to-people links, enables us to attract and persuade other countries to work for the same outcomes as we do, and to deter and enforce in support of our goals. This is a unique and powerful asset, built up over generations. We aim to be the leading soft power nation, using our resources to build the relationships that can project and enhance our influence in the world.

Diplomacy and our global network

5.4   Although we will maintain the ability to defend the UK by force if required, we do not stand alone in confronting threats to our country, our people and interests, and the international order. Our diplomacy will continue to build alliances and partnerships on which we can rely in times of crisis, and to help us to tackle threats at source. Through strong diplomacy we will stay at the heart of the international system, playing a full and active role in the world's leading decision-making bodies, and negotiating political agreements that support our security and our interests. We will continue to shape the global agenda, and to develop and adapt international standards and laws, and the rules-based international order to meet the challenges of the future.

5.5   We will use diplomatic skills and expertise to attract and support our allies, deter our adversaries, and project and amplify the UK's reach and influence. We will continue to develop the best crisis response capability. We will maintain our diplomatic network. **We will extend deep country expertise to wider areas that are vital to our security and prosperity, including language ability in Mandarin and Arabic; and we will extend our expertise on Russia.**

5.6   We administer and fund the Chevening, Marshall and Commonwealth scholarship schemes through DFID and FCO, which create lasting relationships with the global leaders of our current and future partners. **We will fund and administer approximately 2,200 awards a year for young people of high ability to study in the UK through the Chevening, Marshall and Commonwealth scholarship schemes.** We will maximise the benefits of this investment over the coming years, building a strong international network of individuals who support the UK and our values.

5.7   We will continue to promote our 'GREAT Britain' campaign, which showcases what the UK has to offer, and inspires people to visit and to do business, invest and study in the UK. It is the Government's most ambitious international promotional campaign ever, active in 144 countries. It has delivered £1.4 billion for the UK economy, with a further £1.4 billion on track, through higher levels of trade and investment and more people coming to the UK on holiday and to study.

Development

5.8   In 2013, the UK became the first G7 country to spend 0.7% of our GNI on Official Development Assistance – a commitment that we enshrined in law in 2015. DFID is a world-leading organisation, present in 52 countries and committed to research and innovation, transparency and value for money. We are committed to the independence, neutrality and impartiality of our humanitarian assistance, delivered on the basis of need.

5.9   The UK plays a leading role in promoting global development efforts, most recently through the Global Goals for sustainable development agreed at the UN in September 2015. We are also a major contributor to multilateral organisations, such as the UN and the World Bank, and to civil society organisations, including many British charities.

5.10   Our development programme helps to drive economic development and prosperity overseas, enabling a permanent route out of poverty while creating markets for future British business. Our assistance focuses on improving peace, security and governance; equality of opportunity for girls and women; access to basic services for the poorest; and building resilience to crises and responding to disasters when they occur. We promote the golden thread of conditions that drive prosperity all across the world: the rule of law, good governance and the growth of democracy.

5.11   The UK's development assistance also makes a significant contribution to our long-term national security and prosperity. Tackling poverty and instability overseas means tackling the root causes of many of the global challenges that we face including disease, migration and terrorism. DFID will spend at least 50% of its budget on fragile states and regions, including those most directly linked to our national security, in South Asia, the Middle East and Africa. Our new strategy for UK Official Development Assistance will set out our priorities in more detail and ensure that our aid is targeted to deliver more effectively for the world's poorest and for the UK national interest.

Defence engagement

5.12   We are making our defence policy and plans international by design. Our Armed Forces have always operated internationally, deterring major threats, responding to crises and conflicts, and exercising and building defence capabilities together with our allies and partners. We will place more emphasis on being able to operate alongside our allies, including in the UK-France Combined Joint Expeditionary Force, the UK-led Joint Expeditionary Force, and NATO's Very High Readiness Joint Task Force which the UK will lead in 2017.

5.13   Through defence engagement, our Armed Forces help build our understanding and increase our influence in regions that matter to us. Royal Navy ships' visits, for example, are an important way of projecting our soft power. This contributes to our cross-government work overseas to build cooperation to tackle key challenges such as instability, terrorism and extremism, serious and organised crime, and threats to maritime security. Defence engagement also enables faster responses to crises, and promotes our prosperity through support to defence exports.

5.14   As part of this, **we will make defence engagement a funded, core MOD task for the first time**, meaning that the Armed Forces will prioritise defence engagement alongside other core tasks. We will invest in the skills required by opening a new Defence Attaché and Loan Service Centre in the Defence Academy and establishing an Armed Forces defence engagement career stream, making better use of Reservists. **We will also establish British Defence Staffs in the Middle East, Asia Pacific and Africa in 2016**, and increase our institution and capacity building with partners. **We will increase the training we offer to international partners.**

Support to our soft power

5.15   Much of the UK's soft power is completely independent of government, and this is what gives it its strength. In some areas, however, the Government has chosen to invest in people and organisations which play their part in building understanding between countries and promoting the exchange of information and ideas.

5.16   The **British Council** promotes understanding between the UK and the wider world. The Council works in over 100 countries worldwide, and each year reaches over 20 million people face to face and more than 500 million online and via broadcasts and publications. The British Council also provides English language training and expertise around the world, reaching over 200 million people each year. **We will continue to invest in the British Council** to support their programmes targeted at reducing extremism, building skills and promoting institutional reform.

5.17   The **BBC** currently reaches 308 million people worldwide, and its goal is to reach 500 million people by 2022. The **BBC World Service** reaches into some of the most remote places in the world, providing a link to the UK for individuals and societies who would otherwise not have this opportunity. **We will invest £85 million each year by 2017/18 in the BBC's digital, TV and radio services around the world to build the global reach of the World Service and increase access to news and information.**

B. Allies, partners and global engagement

5.18   Strong alliances and partnerships worldwide are more important than ever. In almost every aspect of our national security and prosperity, we must work with others, not because we cannot work alone, but because the threats and opportunities are global.

5.19   Our geostrategic interests and our values are most closely shared with our traditional allies and partners, especially NATO countries, including the US and Canada, European partners, and Australia, New Zealand and Japan. We will invest in these alliances.

5.20   The UK has always sought to maintain and develop political, defence and security, trade, cultural and people-to-people relationships with a wide variety of countries and societies. The development of the Commonwealth over the last fifty years is testament to this. We will build further on our work of the last five years to strengthen security and prosperity partnerships in the Gulf, Africa and Asia Pacific. We will position the UK as a partner for growing powers, to enable us to protect and promote our interests into the future.

5.21   We will not always agree. But direct engagement is an asset to national security as it enables us to improve understanding, address areas of difference, protect our fundamental interests and values, and convince potential adversaries of the benefits of compromise and collaboration.

5.22   We will continue to use our FCO-led global network, and all of our government assets, to develop relationships and to support British individuals, companies and organisations across the world.

The Euro-Atlantic area

5.23   The security and stability of the UK has long depended on our strong partnerships in the Euro-Atlantic area, including NATO. We will deepen our security, intelligence and defence relationships in particular with the US, France and Germany.

North Atlantic Treaty Organization

5.24   NATO is the strongest and most effective military alliance in the world. It has formed the bedrock of our national defence, and of stability in the Euro-Atlantic area, for almost 70 years. Our collective Article 5 commitment, that an armed attack against one state shall be considered an attack on all, underpins the security of the UK and our Allies.

5.25   In September 2014, we hosted the NATO summit in Wales at a point of strategic importance for the Alliance. We set in motion the most significant strengthening of collective defence in a decade, as well as new initiatives to tackle modern security threats. The summit included an unprecedented commitment by 28 Heads of State and Government to halt the decline in defence expenditure. We also hosted over 60 partner countries and launched new joint initiatives to help prevent conflict, build security and enable other countries to draw on NATO's extensive expertise and experience.

5.26   NATO is at the heart of the UK's defence policy. The decisions taken in this National Security Strategy and Strategic Defence and Security Review are informed by NATO's political guidance. The choices we have made to invest in our Special Forces, cyber, Maritime Patrol Aircraft, Intelligence, Surveillance and Reconnaissance aircraft and BMD show our commitment to meeting NATO's highest priority requirements.

5.27   Our defence spending commitment will ensure that we remain NATO's strongest military power in Europe. In 2017 the UK will lead the Very High Readiness Joint Task Force, formed in response to Russia's actions in Ukraine, and we will make a significant contribution to the force every year of this Parliament. As well as providing Typhoons to NATO's Baltic Air Policing mission, we have provided ships and Army units to NATO exercises to reassure our Allies against the threat from Russia, and we will continue to do so. We are joining the German-US Trans-Atlantic Capability Enhancement and Training initiative in the Baltic states and Poland, sharing our military expertise.

5.28   We are working with **Poland** to ensure that the Warsaw Summit in 2016 further strengthens NATO against current threats and adapts it to combat future ones. We will focus on cyber, countering hybrid threats, deterrence including strategic communications, and agile structures and decision-making. We will strongly encourage all our Allies to deliver on their Wales defence investment pledge, and support stronger, more coherent and interoperable NATO partnerships. We will continue to support a robust Alliance response, including in solidarity with **Turkey**, to threats from any direction.

The United States of America

5.29   The US is the leading global economic and defence power, and the world continues to look to it to shape global stability and to lead international responses to crises. The Prime Minister and the President of the United States have recently reaffirmed the essential nature of our special relationship. The US is our pre-eminent partner for security, defence, foreign policy and prosperity. Our contribution to the special relationship includes our European and global reach and influence; intelligence; the strategic location of our Overseas Territories; as well as military interoperability, and the UK's ability to undertake war-fighting independently or as a lead nation in a coalition.

5.30   The US remains the UK's key economic partner. The US is our largest single export partner, with goods and services exports worth £88 billion in 2014, and we are inextricably linked through investment and banking sector channels. As the world's largest economy, the US is vital for global growth and is a key G20 and G7 member, with the Federal Reserve being the central bank for the world's largest reserve currency. It is a key UK ally in developing an effective rules-based global economy. Agreeing and implementing a comprehensive EU-US free trade agreement could boost the UK economy by up to £10 billion annually.

5.31   The unparalleled extent of UK-US cooperation on nuclear, intelligence, diplomacy, technology and military capabilities plays a major role in guaranteeing our national security. Our ability to operate together in future is at the heart of our planning. The UK and the US are at the centre of NATO's collective defence and security, including through the declaration of our nuclear capabilities to the defence of the Alliance.

5.32   **We will strengthen the interoperability with the US of our Armed Forces so that they are better able to work together when required through regularly planning and training together.** Collaboration on our aircraft carrier programmes and the F35 Lightning, including the US decision to base aircraft in the UK, will enable us to fly aircraft from each other's ships, and work together on operating them from the land and at sea. Our investment in P8 Maritime Patrol Aircraft will enable us to provide protection to each other's aircraft carriers and further improve our interoperability in anti-submarine warfare, while also providing efficiencies in basing and support. We will also work very closely to optimise the use of strategically important capabilities such as Special Forces, cyber, Intelligence, Surveillance and Reconnaissance, and satellite communications.

5.33　We work together to support peace and stability in Europe's neighbourhood, the Middle East, Africa and Central Asia. **We will work with the US to deliver more for global stability and our shared interests:**

- We will extend our cooperation on global issues, especially countering violent extremism and terrorism, corruption, climate change, and promoting the rule of law and free trade, including through conclusion of the transformational Transatlantic Trade and Investment Partnership.

- We will enhance our cooperation on development in fragile states and regions, building on the new joint DFID-USAID programmes to support education in countries affected by conflict.

France

5.34　The UK and France are the two European nations with the full range of military capabilities and the political will to protect our interests globally. We have built an exceptionally close defence and security relationship with France through the Lancaster House Treaty of 2010. We work together to help build the rule of law, security and stability in the Middle East and Africa, to counter terrorism, extremism and organised crime, on aviation security, and on disaster relief and evacuation operations in areas of mutual interest.

5.35　**We will further strengthen the UK-France defence and security relationship.** Our Combined Joint Expeditionary Force, which will be operational in 2016, will provide a potent combined reaction force of up to 10,000 personnel available to plan for and respond to crises, including beyond Europe. We are working with the French Navy to ensure that we exploit the shared opportunities when the Royal Navy's aircraft carriers come into service. The Army's high readiness 16 Air Assault Brigade is developing strong links with its French counterparts. Our air forces work closely together on operations in the Middle East and North Africa. We are also working together on how our militaries can further contribute to domestic security in our respective countries.

5.36　We are also expanding our equipment collaboration, including through the development of a joint future Unmanned Combat Air System programme and Maritime Mine Counter Measure demonstrator, procurement and development of missiles, and maximising common supply chain efficiencies. We will continue developing our joint nuclear facilities in France and the UK.

Germany

5.37　Germany is an essential partner, given its economic power and growing influence on international security. It plays a major role in Afghanistan, has helped lead the European response to Russia's actions in Ukraine, and has missions delivering security in the Middle East, Balkans, and Africa. We strongly support Germany's bid to become a permanent member of an expanded United Nations Security Council.

5.38　**We will work to intensify our security and defence relationship with Germany.** We will deepen our intelligence sharing and collaboration on tackling terrorist threats, and work more closely on energy security, military support to humanitarian and development work, cyber and capacity building in countries outside Europe. We will also work more closely together to strengthen NATO, including the capabilities of its European members. We will strengthen our cooperation on operations, missions and training as well as enhance interoperability, such as between our navies and armies. We will work to deepen our cooperation on equipment, enhancing capabilities and reducing the support costs of common aircraft (Typhoon and A400M). We are also exploring future equipment collaboration. While we still intend to withdraw our forces from Germany by 2020, we will continue to seek opportunities to train alongside the German Armed Forces.

European partners

5.39   We will strengthen our defence links with all NATO and EU partners, including **Italy**, with whom we have longstanding procurement and operational cooperation, and **Spain**, with whom we are working closely on the new NATO Very High Readiness Joint Task Force. Complementing our work in NATO, the Joint Expeditionary Force is a UK-led collaboration involving **Norway**, **the Netherlands**, **Denmark**, **Estonia**, **Latvia** and **Lithuania**. Together, we are improving our ability to respond quickly to crises unilaterally or as part of a wider coalition. We are also working with our partners in the Northern Group, notably **Poland**, **Sweden** and **Finland**, to promote more effective defence cooperation in northern Europe.

The European Union

5.40   A secure and prosperous Europe is essential for a secure and prosperous UK. We want Europe to be dynamic, competitive and outwardly focused, delivering prosperity and security.

5.41   Through its 28 member states and EU institutions, the EU has a range of capabilities to build security and respond to threats, which can be complementary to those of NATO. These include sanctions, missions (military and civilian), and security and development support worldwide. Recent examples include sanctions imposed on Russia, assistance in Ukraine, and Operation Sophia, which tackles people smuggling in the Mediterranean. Operation Sophia, the UK-commanded Operation Atalanta which counters piracy off the Horn of Africa and Operation Althea which provides capacity-building and training in the Balkans are examples of successful Common Security and Defence Policy operations. The UK has played a leading role in them, ensuring that the EU's work supports UK priorities. The UK also plays an active role in the EU Civil Protection Mechanism which coordinates assistance to victims of disasters.

5.42   We will also continue to foster closer coordination and cooperation between the EU and other institutions, principally NATO, in ways which support our national priorities and build Euro-Atlantic security. This will include areas such as cyber and countering hybrid threats, and work to develop security capacity in other states. We will form a cross-Whitehall joint Euro-Atlantic Security Policy Unit to bring together diplomatic and defence expertise on this.

5.43   The EU, and euro area in particular, is the UK's biggest trading partner, and the financial ties between the UK and the euro area are strong. The EU accounts for 44% of UK exports of goods and services and 53% of UK imports of goods and services. Over 80% of UK firms that trade do business with the EU.

5.44   We are negotiating with our partners to agree **EU reforms** that will make it more competitive, flexible and democratically accountable, to benefit all 28 member states and to address the concerns of the British people. This would make the EU a stronger partner for economies around the world that want to invest. We will hold a referendum on our membership of the EU by the end of 2017.

Eastern neighbourhood

5.45   **Russia**'s illegal annexation of Crimea and destabilising activities in Ukraine directly challenge European security and the rules-based international order. We are working in

NATO, the EU and the UN to ensure that Russia is held to account for its actions. We are working with EU partners to maintain the pressure of sanctions on Russia to comply with the commitments it entered into at the Minsk Summit, withdraw from Crimea, and meet its international obligations in respect of the rule of law, human rights and democracy. We will continue to take firm steps to maintain peace and security.

5.46   We also want to keep open the possibility of cooperation. We will continue to seek to engage with Russia on global security, including international efforts to tackle the ISIL threat, building on the successful cooperation that we shared in negotiations on Iran's nuclear programme.

5.47   We support a diplomatic resolution of the crisis in **Ukraine** and will continue to work to uphold Ukraine's sovereignty, assist its people and build resilience. We have provided humanitarian aid, and we will continue to support Ukraine with advice and assistance on fighting corruption, defence reform and training their Armed Forces. We will continue to support the EU Assistance Mission which the UK was instrumental in launching, as part of a wider package of support from the EU.

5.48   The threats of both state-sponsored and non-state actors undermining the security and stability of the Western Balkans and Eastern neighbourhood are likely to endure. We will continue to work with NATO and the EU, as well as bilaterally, to build greater resilience in the region, including through our programme to support governance and economic reforms, tackle terrorism and extremism, and deal with migration challenges. We will continue to support the EU's peacekeeping operation in Bosnia. This mission, which uses NATO Headquarters, makes an important contribution to peace and stability in the Western Balkans.

5.49   The **Organization for Security and Cooperation in Europe (OSCE)**, the largest regional security organisation in the world, plays an important role in crisis and conflict resolution. We will use our influence as a leading member to develop the OSCE's role in Ukraine, and support the OSCE's work on conventional arms control, confidence and security building measures, and democracy and human rights with all 56 participating states, including Russia.

The wider world

The Commonwealth

5.50   The Commonwealth is a worldwide partnership of diversity and shared values. We will work with the new Secretary-General to strengthen the Commonwealth's promotion of democratic values, development, and trade and investment and to address extremism and radicalisation, corruption and climate change. We will strengthen partnerships with Commonwealth countries around the world, as described later in this section.

5.51   Our strong bilateral defence and security relationship with **Australia** reflects a modern partnership which addresses issues of common concern. We are partners in the Five Eyes and Five Power Defence Arrangements and share common interests in the Asia-Pacific region. Our relationship is underpinned by the 2013 Defence and Security Cooperation Treaty, and we have annual meetings of foreign and defence ministers (AUKMIN) through which we coordinate responses to security challenges such as ISIL. Since March 2014, the UK has operated alongside Australia on the two Malaysian airline incidents, Ebola in Sierra Leone and disaster relief in Vanuatu; and we continue to work closely on counter-ISIL operations in Iraq.

We will cooperate in developing new capabilities while working together to address global challenges and strengthen the rules-based international order.

5.52   The UK and **Canada** are the only two nations to be members of the G7, the Five Eyes community, NATO and the Commonwealth. We have a broad range of shared interests, our diplomats share facilities in a number of countries and our Armed Forces work seamlessly together. The UK's strong economic relationship with Canada will be boosted by the implementation of Canada-EU Comprehensive Economic and Trade Agreement.

5.53   We work closely with **New Zealand** in a range of defence and security areas, including the anti-ISIL coalition. Our mutual understanding and cooperation is supported by an annual foreign policy Strategic Dialogue and a Joint Statement on Defence Cooperation.

The Five Eyes community

5.54   The UK's security and prosperity is also underpinned by our cooperation with Australia, Canada, New Zealand and the US through the Five Eyes intelligence sharing partnership; the Five Eyes Law Enforcement Group on reducing the international threat and impact of organised crime; and the Consular Colloque which allows us to support each other in protecting our respective nationals overseas. We will strengthen our cooperation in these areas.

Middle East and North Africa

5.55   The region to the south of our European neighbourhood is a significant source of both threat and opportunity, and will remain vital to our national security and prosperity. We will continue to devote significant resources to building the relationships we need in this region, and to tackling the threats from it.

5.56   The UK's relations with the six Gulf Cooperation Council (GCC) states (**Bahrain, Kuwait, Oman, Qatar, Saudi Arabia**, and the **United Arab Emirates**) are broad and deep. They are vital partners for the UK in working towards sustainable, long-term regional stability, in addressing direct threats to the UK from terrorism, extremism and organised crime, and for our energy security. We cooperate on countering ISIL and other terrorist groups, promoting stability across the Middle East and North Africa, and providing humanitarian assistance to those most in need, while continuing to address issues on which our views differ. We encourage greater trade and investment in both directions. We are working with Gulf and international partners to end the conflict in **Yemen** through an inclusive political settlement.

5.57   **We will set out our vision of our future relationships with partners in the region in our new Gulf Strategy.** In particular, **we will build a permanent and more substantial UK military presence** to reflect our historic relationships, the long-term nature of both challenges and opportunities and to reassure our Gulf allies. We have begun work on a new naval base in Bahrain, HMS Juffair, to support Royal Navy deployments in the region, and we will establish a new British Defence Staff in the Middle East.

5.58   We will ensure that our Ministerial engagement is regular and sustained. We will broaden our cooperation and work to improve GCC capacity in areas which support their security and resilience, and ours. We will underpin this through cooperation in areas ranging from rule of law to education, healthcare and infrastructure. Recognising their significance for wider regional stability, we will deepen our partnerships with regional aid institutions.

5.59   We will use all resources across government and continue to play a leading role in the global coalition of over 60 nations to defeat ISIL and violent extremism. We are conducting air strikes against ISIL forces in Iraq and co-leading work to undermine ISIL's funding streams and to curb the flow of foreign fighters. Defeating ISIL will require a long-term commitment to promote stability, inclusive political solutions and prosperity in the region.

5.60   We will continue to work in support of a more secure, stable, united and prosperous **Iraq**, with the capacity to provide security and opportunities for its people, tackle extremism and support regional stability. We are working closely with the Iraqi government to address the political root causes of the current conflict and supporting the implementation of political reforms.

5.61   We are supporting those with a moderate and unified vision for **Syria**. Through EU sanctions, we have put pressure on the Assad regime and its supporters. We will provide emergency sanctuary for up to 20,000 security-vetted displaced Syrians during this Parliament. The UK has already committed over £1.1 billion in aid in response to the Syrian crisis, second only to the US, and will increase this commitment next year. We will also increase our support to **Lebanon** and **Jordan** to reinforce their security and help them deal with the mass influx of refugees. In 2016, the UK will co-host an international conference on Syria to deliver a significant shift in the provision of immediate and longer-term support to refugees and host communities, with a focus on education and jobs.

5.62   After more than a decade of negotiations, we and partners reached a historic deal in July this year that will impose strict limits and inspections on **Iran**'s nuclear programme. The international community will now lift some of its sanctions on Iran. We will encourage Iran to play a transparent and constructive role in regional affairs, particularly in the struggle against violent Islamist extremism. This is an example of the progress that can be made through diplomacy and dialogue, and provides lessons for clear-eyed engagement.

5.63   We will take every opportunity to promote a peaceful two-state solution through the **Middle East Peace Process**, as the only way to secure lasting peace.

5.64   We have been working to support **Libya**'s transition to democracy since the 2011 revolution, in particular in 2014/15 through UN-led efforts to broker political agreement between warring parties and to enable a new constitution to be agreed. We and the international community stand ready to support the Libyan people and the leaders that they choose in their fight against the terrorism that threatens them and us. We stand ready to help Libya address the challenges of transition.

5.65   We want to see long-term stability and security across **North Africa** and will continue to work with partners, including the EU, to support this. We will expand our promotion of good governance. We will work to deliver a stronger bilateral relationship with **Egypt**, focusing on promoting reform, security cooperation and prosperity. With **Algeria**, we will support good governance and energy security. In **Tunisia**, our cooperation focuses on security, particularly after the terrorist attacks in Sousse, and economic reform, and in **Morocco** we support good governance, business and cultural links.

Sub-Saharan Africa

5.66   Africa is increasingly a continent of opportunity, and economic and political potential, despite challenges from instability and poverty. The UK has strong historical, people-to-people and business links. Over the next five years, we aim to deepen the UK's relationships with African countries significantly. To enable this, we will deliver a more strategic and coordinated government approach to Africa.

5.67   We are committed to Africa's development. We will continue to make substantial investments to promote greater economic growth and poverty reduction. We will work closely with African countries and institutions, as well as with development partners including the US and France.

5.68   The UK will continue to play a leadership role in helping to tackle the threat of terrorism to the region. In **Somalia**, we work closely with our partners to increase their capacity to combat terrorism, including through training security forces and boosting aviation security. We also command the EU's counter-piracy operation in the region. We will seek to strengthen international support to the **Nigerian** authorities to tackle terrorism. We are expanding our British Military Advisory and Training Team and increasing the number of Short Term Training Teams to help deliver more training and capacity building support to the Nigerian Armed Forces. In **Kenya**, the British Peace Support Team assists the East Africa Standby Force and trains Kenyan, Ethiopian and Ugandan forces in regional peacekeeping, as well as coordinating the UK military contribution to Somalia. Our Armed Forces will continue to use training areas in Kenya, supported by the British Army Training Unit Kenya. With **South Africa**, the British Peace Support Team assists the Southern Africa Development Community forces including in Malawi and Zambia and supports military reform in South Africa.

5.69   We have strengthened our commitment to international peacekeeping in Africa, and will make new deployments to UN missions in Somalia and South Sudan. We will work with African partners to help to ensure that the lessons of the Ebola outbreak are learned, and local resilience is strengthened for the future.

5.70   The **African Union** (AU) has unique legitimacy as a pan-African institution. It has taken a leading role with the UN and EU in peacekeeping and peace enforcement in Somalia and the Central African Republic, and against Boko Haram, and is an important political player in Sudan and South Sudan. We work with the AU to promote progressive values, including on peacekeeping, conflict resolution, migration, governance and trade. This year we provided £30 million through the European Development Fund to the Africa Peace Facility. We will continue to work closely with the AU on building stability, and will increase our engagement on trade and development.

Asia and the Pacific

5.71   The Asia-Pacific region has significant economic opportunities for the UK, and considerable influence on the future integrity and credibility of the rules-based international order. We will continue to work with like-minded partners in the region, including **Japan**, Australia, New Zealand and others to defend and protect our global shared interests, uphold the rules-based international order and to strengthen cooperation on settling international and regional disputes.

5.72   We are strengthening considerably our defence, political and diplomatic cooperation with Japan, our closest security partner in Asia, as they take an increasingly global outlook on security issues. We strongly support Japan's bid to become a permanent member of an expanded United Nations Security Council, and support Japan taking a greater role in UN peacekeeping. We will build on our defence cooperation, based on successful operational cooperation including on counter-piracy in the Gulf of Aden and off Somalia. We will collaborate further, particularly on disaster relief operations and broader joint deployments both regionally and worldwide. We will continue to explore longer term opportunities for closer defence engagement and defence industrial collaboration. As the world's third largest economy, the Japanese market continues to provide important trade and investment opportunities for the UK.

5.73   We will also deepen our cooperation with the **Republic of Korea**, including in maritime and cyber security, countering violent extremism and terrorism, and climate change.

5.74   Our relationship with **China** is rapidly expanding. We do not expect to agree with the Chinese Government on everything. In all our dealings we will protect the UK's interests vigorously. But our aim is to **build a deeper partnership with China, working more closely together to address global challenges**, including climate change, AMR, terrorism, economic development in Africa, peacekeeping, and to counter North Korea's nuclear programme. We strongly support China's greater integration into more of the world's key institutions and organisations as its global role and responsibilities grow. The UK and China will establish a high level security dialogue to strengthen exchanges and cooperation on security issues such as non-proliferation, organised crime, cyber crime and illegal immigration. The agreement on cyber-enabled commercial espionage, announced during the Chinese State Visit in October 2015, shows the progress being made. We will work together to strengthen cooperation on settling international and regional disputes peacefully in accordance with the UN Charter and international law.

5.75   We are also strengthening our economic relationship with China, as set out in Chapter 6. Our ambition is that China becomes our second biggest export destination within the next decade. In addition we aim to establish London as the leading global centre for renminbi products and services, across banking, asset management and insurance.

5.76   **India** is the world's largest democracy. We are working with India to deepen our bilateral partnership. This includes a closer strategic partnership on diplomatic, defence and security issues, including terrorism, extremism, cyber, nuclear proliferation, and conflict. We are working together to strengthen our people to people links, culture, education, skills, science, technology, research and innovation; to address the challenges of climate change; and to ensure clean energy supplies. This partnership will be reinforced by biennial meetings of our Prime Ministers. **We will champion an EU-India Free Trade Agreement to help make it easier for UK companies to do business in India**, create Smart City partnerships between Indian and UK cities, and share UK skills with the growing Indian workforce through new centres in India. We strongly support India's bid to become a permanent member of an expanded United Nations Security Council.

5.77   In January 2015, after 13 years of combat operations came to a close, NATO started its new training and advising mission in **Afghanistan**. Today, the Afghan security forces are responsible for delivering security across their own country. Through our work at the Afghan National Army Officer Academy, we are helping to develop the next generation of Afghanistan's military leaders. Our Armed Forces are also advising the Afghan security ministries, and are playing an important role in NATO's Resolute Support Mission Headquarters.

5.78   Although the UK's combat mission has ended, we continue to support the National Unity Government of Afghanistan as they seek to build a more peaceful, secure and prosperous future for the country. We have made long-term commitments to Afghanistan's future, including through financial aid and political support, which helps Afghanistan to make continued progress on corruption, good governance and human rights. Our bilateral aid programme – £178 million this year – will help set the conditions for long-term stability.

5.79   **Pakistan**'s stability is important for UK interests, and we have strong people-to-people links. We will work with Pakistan to promote economic stability, growth and jobs, deliver more inclusive public services and make democracy work. We support Pakistan's efforts to tackle terrorism and defeat extremism, and have a shared interest in seeing a stable country with more constructive relations with its neighbours.

5.80   We have strong historical ties, a large diaspora community in the UK and a significant development partnership with **Bangladesh**. We will work with them to lower levels of poverty, build resilience and counter the drivers of violent extremism. We have a close relationship with **Nepal** through the 200 years of Gurkha service.

5.81   We will strengthen engagement with the ten member states of the **Association of South East Asian Nations** (ASEAN), including through coordinated humanitarian aid and disaster relief, and we will cooperate on issues such as countering violent extremism and terrorism, particularly with **Indonesia** and **Malaysia**. Our defence garrison in **Brunei**, funded by His Majesty the Sultan, underpins a strong bilateral relationship, while providing a major permanent UK military presence in the region. The Government supports restarting discussions for an EU-ASEAN trade agreement, which could be worth £3 billion to the UK economy, and pursuing negotiations on a country-by-country basis as building towards that goal.

5.82   The **Five Power Defence Arrangements** between the UK, Australia, New Zealand, Malaysia and **Singapore** are an important part of our commitment to peace and security in the region. We will increase our contribution, in particular through exercises, including with our new aircraft carriers, and joint training, and continue to invest in our strong bilateral defence relationships.

Latin America and the Caribbean

5.83   Latin America is increasingly important to our security and prosperity and we have built good relationships with **Brazil** and **Mexico**, the region's rising powers, as well as with the other innovative, open economies of the Pacific Alliance, **Chile**, **Peru** and **Colombia**. We will increase our cooperation with Brazil on education and skills, green growth, energy security, infrastructure, defence sales, countering organised crime, cyber and science and technology, and by progressing EU-Mercosur trade agreements. We strongly support Brazil's bid to become a permanent member of an expanded United Nations Security Council.

5.84   We are deepening our defence relationship with Mexico, and through high-level bilateral talks we are promoting free trade and open markets. We will also increase support on justice reform, rule of law and human rights. In **Belize** we are re-establishing the Army's jungle training centre. We will work with countries across the region on law enforcement and justice to improve their ability to tackle the dangerous narcotics trade.

5.85   We will continue to encourage the new government of **Argentina** to respect the rules-based international order, particularly in relation to the Falkland Islands.

5.86   We have extensive links to the **Caribbean** through our five Overseas Territories and the eight Commonwealth Caribbean countries. Every year, 800,000 British nationals visit the region, and the UK is the top export destination for much of the Caribbean. We are investing £300 million in infrastructure and launching a new UK-Caribbean Infrastructure Partnership to help drive growth and development and create trade and investment opportunities for the UK. We will continue to work together on health, justice and disaster resilience, including by investing £30 million to help ensure that hospitals remain operational when natural disasters strike.

C. Strengthening the rules-based international order and its institutions

5.87   The UK was a leading architect of the current system of institutions and relations, and we have been at the forefront of its expansion since the end of the Cold War – for example, extending the reach and scope of international justice through the establishment of the International Criminal Court. We have helped to shape the norms that govern use of force, prevent conflict, advance human rights and good governance, promote open and fair international trade relations and support freedom of navigation.

5.88   The rules-based international order must continue to adapt to a changing world, including to the needs of new and growing powers. We will work with allies and partners to strengthen and adapt existing institutions and rules so that they remain representative and effective. We will seek to extend the benefits of the rules-based international order by encouraging and supporting greater cooperation on global challenges.

Institutions

5.89   Multilateral institutions set and enforce rules and standards of behaviour, and deliver assistance and capacity-building programmes across a wide range of areas essential to the UK's interests.

United Nations

5.90   The UN is the world's leading multilateral institution. The UK is a founding member and we take seriously our responsibility towards ensuring its effectiveness and legitimacy. We support UN Security Council reform, including permanent seats for Brazil, Germany, India and Japan, and permanent African representation.

5.91   The UN is only as effective as its member states are willing to allow. We will ensure that our funding is used to strengthen the UN's efficiency and capacity to work towards the goals that we all share. We will focus our political, diplomatic, military and development resources to help the UN to contribute to the Global Goals for sustainable development; implement the UN Secretary General's Action Plan on Preventing Violent Extremism; strengthen UN conflict prevention and mediation, peacebuilding capacity, and work on human rights; deliver a better and more coordinated global humanitarian response; and support the World Health Organization in recognising and responding more rapidly to global health emergencies.

5.92   Peacekeeping is one of the UN's most important roles. The UK will continue to champion reform to increase the efficiency and impact of UN engagement. **We will double the number of military personnel that we contribute to UN peacekeeping operations.** We will also increase UK law enforcement and civilian experts on UN peace operations and in UN headquarters, and we will continue to train international peacekeepers. We will form a cross-Whitehall joint UN Peacekeeping Policy Unit to maximise our military and civilian impact.

Global Economic Architecture

5.93   International Financial Institutions (IFIs) play an essential role in securing strong, balanced and sustainable economic growth, safeguarding global economic and financial stability, promoting economic inclusion and reducing poverty around the world. They set rules and standards, and offer policy advice, technical assistance and financing instruments across a very wide range of areas, which benefit their global memberships. The IFIs are therefore central to our work to promote prosperity for the UK and globally, as described in Chapter 6, and we are a major shareholder in and large contributor to them. We are committed to their ongoing success and timely adaptation to new economic, financial and institutional contexts.

5.94 We will work to build the inclusivity of the IFIs' membership and decision-making, so they continue to command credibility and legitimacy in the eyes of their members. This is central to their lasting efficacy. In particular:

- The **International Monetary Fund** agreed reforms in 2010 to enhance the voice of emerging markets and developing countries. The UK was one of the first members to make the statutory changes to put the deal into effect, and remains committed to its full implementation.

- We also support reform of the **World Bank** to adapt its operations more effectively to individual countries, particularly fragile states.

5.95 The **G20** is the premier forum for international economic cooperation. We support its increased activism and global leadership to achieve strong, sustainable growth, coordinating macro-economic policy and tackling the challenges which could threaten this goal. We also welcome the continued close working of the **G7**, a forum made up of nations with shared values, interests and global outlooks. The G7 has coordinated action on climate change and global health security, among other issues of global importance. We will continue to work closely with partners to coordinate action, agree positions and reinforce each other in international negotiations.

5.96 We will continue to work with partners in the **World Trade Organization** to integrate developing countries into the open, transparent and rules-based trading system.

Standards and laws

5.97 The UK is committed to strengthening and enforcing existing standards and laws, and adapting them to address new challenges.

5.98 The **International Court of Justice (ICJ)** is the primary mechanism by which states are able to settle disputes peacefully. As part of our commitment to the rule of law in international relations, the UK accepts the compulsory jurisdiction of the ICJ. The **International Criminal Court (ICC)** plays an important role in global efforts to end impunity for the most serious crimes of international concern, including genocide, war crimes and crimes against humanity. We support the ICC as a court of last resort when others are unwilling or unable to prosecute perpetrators, and we support its investigative and judicial processes. We will continue to seek ways to support the ICC and other tribunals to increase their efficiency and effectiveness.

5.99 International economic sanctions have proved their effectiveness as part of wider efforts to uphold agreements and laws, and inflict a cost on those who breach them. Sanctions, including those coordinated through the EU, helped bring Iran to the negotiating table and are an essential element of our response to Russia's actions in Ukraine. To improve the UK's implementation and enforcement of financial sanctions, we are establishing an Office of Financial Sanctions Implementation and introducing legislation to increase penalties for financial sanctions evasion. **We will review sanctions governance to ensure the best coordination of policy, implementation and enforcement.**

Counter proliferation

5.100 Rules and norms to counter the proliferation of illicit arms and weapons of mass destruction play a vital role in our security. The UK has consistently been at the forefront of international efforts to tackle proliferation. We devote substantial efforts to this, and will continue to do so.

5.101 We will continue to support the implementation of the Joint Comprehensive Plan of Action with Iran. The international safeguards regime which underpins Iran's commitment to enhanced verification and inspections will give the international community confidence that Iran's nuclear programme is, and will remain, exclusively peaceful. If at any time Iran fails to meet its commitments under the Joint Comprehensive Plan of Action, international sanctions will be re-imposed.

5.102 We will maintain pressure on Syria to comply fully with its obligations under the Chemical Weapons Convention. We will support the mechanisms established by the **UN Security Council** and **Organisation for the Prohibition of Chemical Weapons** to ensure that all those responsible for the use of chemical weapons in Syria are held to account.

5.103 We will focus our efforts at the final Nuclear Security Summit in 2016 on reducing the risk of nuclear material and information falling into the hands of terrorists and criminals, including by working towards the full implementation of global standards for maintaining the security of nuclear material. We will support the **International Atomic Energy Agency** as they take on a greater leadership role after the Summit has concluded.

5.104 We remain committed to the Nuclear Non-Proliferation Treaty, and to the creation of a Middle East Zone free from nuclear weapons and all other weapons of mass destruction. We will continue to campaign for successful negotiations on a Fissile Material Cut-Off Treaty in the Conference on Disarmament, the entry into force of the Comprehensive Test Ban Treaty and universal membership of the Chemical Weapons Convention and the Biological and Toxin Weapons Convention.

5.105 Over the last five years, the UK has led the international community to agreement on a new Arms Trade Treaty. **We will campaign to increase the number of countries that have ratified the Arms Trade Treaty.**

Human rights

5.106 Our long-term security and prosperity depend on the rules-based international order upholding our values. Security and prosperity suffer when violations and abuses of human rights go unchecked. Over the last five years, we have stood up for what we believe in: intervening to stop a massacre in Libya, leading the world in tackling sexual violence in conflict, and helping people who have fled violence in Syria.

5.107 We will continue to promote universal human rights as an integral part of building prosperity and stability around the world. We will work with our partners to strengthen the promotion and protection of human rights, and hold to account those responsible for the worst violations and abuses. This is part of our work to promote the golden thread of democracy, rule of law, free media and open, accountable institutions.

International humanitarian law

5.108 Current conflicts are characterised by the growing influence of non-state armed groups, violence against civilians and denial of access for humanitarian workers. The UK has a strong history of upholding international humanitarian law. We will continue to lead by example, including supporting the International Committee of the Red Cross to strengthen compliance with the Geneva Conventions.

5.109 We will use UN mechanisms such as the Responsibility to Protect, Rights Up Front, the Human Rights Council, and the Children in Armed Conflict agenda to drive global change, in line with British values.

5.110 We will underpin our advocacy with practical support to tribunals, governments, NGOs and the Red Cross Movement in upholding and enforcing international criminal and humanitarian law.

5.111 We will work with governments to build more accountable defence and security forces that uphold international humanitarian law, through our international education and training programmes.

Women, peace and security

5.112 The full attainment of political, social and economic rights for women is one of the greatest prizes of the 21st century, and central to greater peace and stability overseas.

5.113 This is a UK priority, and we will ensure that women's rights are fully taken into account in our overseas counter-extremism work, in humanitarian emergencies, in our early warning and conflict analysis, and in our new military doctrine. We will continue to promote the active participation of women in peace-building discussions, including through work with governments such as in Afghanistan and Iraq.

5.114 This is already a key theme running through our development work. We will build on it over the next five years, including through investing in research to understand what needs to be done in conflict-affected states to ensure lasting equality for women and girls.

Preventing Sexual Violence in Conflict Initiative

5.115 The UK led the world with the Preventing Sexual Violence in Conflict Initiative. We will expand its reach and implementation, focusing on Iraq and Syria. Working with the UN, AU and other multilateral bodies as well as supportive governments around the world, we will do even more to tackle impunity for sexual violence crimes, secure widespread implementation of the International Protocol on the Documentation and Investigation of Sexual Violence in Conflict, and encourage greater international support for survivors.

D. Tackling conflict and building stability overseas

5.116 Instability, conflict and state failure overseas pose an increasingly direct threat to the UK. They create large-scale humanitarian and development need, drive global migration and hamper economic growth, and result in ungoverned spaces which can be exploited by terrorists and criminals. It is firmly in our national security interests to tackle the causes and to mitigate the effects of conflict.

5.117 The UK has the will and ability to work in the most fragile places; can bring substantial resources and expertise to bear; and is home to world-leading civil society organisations. We established ourselves as a global leader through our comprehensive 2011 Building Stability Overseas Strategy, which covers early warning, crisis response and prevention, coordinated through NSC-led strategies for countries and regions at risk of instability. When crises hit, our investment of 0.7% of our GNI on overseas development means that we can respond rapidly.

5.118 In this Parliament we will deliver an even more ambitious approach. We will substantially increase our investment in fragile states and regions:

- **We will spend at least 50% of DFID's budget in fragile states and regions in every year of this Parliament.** This is a major investment in global stability, including in regions of strategic importance to the UK, such as the Middle East and South Asia.

- We launched a new £1 billion Conflict, Stability and Security Fund in April 2015, replacing the Conflict Pool. Under NSC direction, the Conflict, Stability and Security Fund provides a greater link between strategic decision-making and action on the ground, and in directing cross-government departmental effort in fragile states. **We will increase the Conflict, Stability and Security Fund from £1 billion in 2015/16 to over £1.3 billion a year by 2019/20.** This will increase our capacity to prevent threats and build stability, as well as respond to crises more quickly and effectively. The Conflict, Stability and Security Fund will have more resources and expertise to address the drivers of transnational threats to stability such as extremism, illegal migration and serious and organised crime.

5.119 Our approach requires a consolidated, whole-of-government effort, using our diplomatic, development, defence and law enforcement capabilities, as well as drawing on external expertise. Our innovative, expanded civil-military Stabilisation Unit will continue to support more effective cross-government crisis response, stabilisation and conflict prevention in fragile states.

5.120 This requires patient, long-term work. Success depends on strong local, national and regional partnerships, and on a rules-based international order which provides the framework in which a society can develop the strong and legitimate institutions it needs to manage tensions peacefully.

Tackling the drivers of instability

5.121 We will help to address the causes of conflict and instability through increased support for tackling corruption, promoting good governance, developing security and justice, and creating jobs and economic opportunity. These are essential elements of the golden thread of democracy and development, supporting more peaceful and inclusive societies.

5.122 The UK will hold a global anti-corruption summit in London in 2016 to generate commitments and resources to end impunity, strengthen the ability of international institutions to tackle corruption, and develop ways for citizens to challenge corruption. We are already investing more than £190 million over three years to help developing countries investigate and prosecute corruption, and hold governments to account. We will invest further over this Parliament in tackling corruption, illicit financial flows and tax evasion, and to improve transparency in poor countries. We have created a new international anti-corruption unit in the NCA, with £21 million committed up to 2020 to recover funds stolen from developing countries and prosecute those responsible.

5.123 We will increase cross-departmental security and justice assistance through the Conflict, Stability and Security Fund. In particular, we will help fragile countries to access the best of British legal, policing and security expertise, including through our new Joint International Policing Hub.

5.124 We will significantly increase our investment to support more effective and accountable institutions at all levels. As part of this, **we will double the existing Good Governance Fund to support economic and governance reforms in the eastern European neighbourhood to £40 million per year by the end of this Parliament.** We will increase our governance work in North Africa, providing new support to countries and communities to improve inclusion and stability.

Migration

5.125 Tackling conflict and improving stability and economic opportunity overseas is part of our long-term, comprehensive approach to migration. We will ensure that our investment in countries of origin helps to reduce forced displacement and migration over the long term. We will do much more to help refugees closer to their homes. We will deliver humanitarian aid to those who are forcibly displaced, and provide education and livelihood opportunities. We will build the capacity of source and transit countries to manage their borders more effectively, and to tackle organised immigration crime.

Stronger early warning and crisis response

5.126 Early warning and rapid crisis response remain central to our efforts to prevent, mitigate and resolve conflict and instability overseas. We will implement a new early warning and early action system across government. We will respond more rapidly to crises overseas through more pre-trained staff in departments across government, a larger standby capacity, and more joint departmental training and exercises. We will increase our contingency funding to enable more flexible and rapid delivery of programmes. We will harness the expertise of the UK's world-leading scientists and researchers to strengthen resilience and crisis response in developing countries.

5.127 We will establish a DFID/MOD fast track mechanism to speed up the deployment of military assets and expertise for rapid crisis response when no civilian alternative is available, in line with Oslo guidelines on the use of military and civil defence assets in disaster relief in another country.

Building international resilience

5.128 Our long-term objective is to strengthen the resilience of poor and fragile countries to disasters, shocks and climate change. This will save lives and reduce the risk of instability. It is also much better value for money to invest in disaster preparedness and resilience than to respond after the event.

5.129 We will play a leading role in delivering the International Agreement for Disaster Risk Reduction, agreed in March 2015, to improve the resilience of partner nations to cope with crises. This will draw on the UK's expertise in crisis management in government, the private sector and academia.

5.130 We have chosen to invest in and lead international work on two major areas of global risk which threaten stability overseas and the UK's long-term security: climate change and health security.

Climate change

5.131 Climate change is one of the biggest long-term challenges for the future of our planet. It leads to and exacerbates instability overseas, including through resource stresses, migration, impact on trade, and global economic and food insecurity.

5.132 We set up the International Climate Fund to provide £3.87 billion in international climate finance between April 2011 and March 2016, helping the world's poorest to adapt to climate change and promote cleaner, greener growth. **We will increase UK climate finance for developing countries by at least 50%, rising to £5.8 billion over five years**, to reduce emissions, increase access to energy, build resilience of the poorest and most vulnerable people, and reduce deforestation. This will in turn help reduce global impacts and reduce the costs of responding to disasters.

5.133 We will continue to focus diplomatic effort on driving global action to reduce emissions through national policies, bilateral cooperation and negotiations under the UN Framework Convention on Climate Change. We will work with partners to manage the consequences of climate change, including for our strategic interests such as in the Polar regions.

5.134 Our businesses, institutions and public bodies are world leaders in tackling and adapting to climate change. We will support them in exploring opportunities to export UK expertise to countries developing their own mitigation and adaptation policies.

Global health security

5.135 Health crises can have regional and international impact. Diseases can spread rapidly, including across borders. The emergence of drug-resistant disease is an increasing global threat. A comprehensive approach overseas and at home is critical to protect British nationals and our wider interests, and to mitigate the impact of health threats in other countries.

5.136 We will build on our international action to strengthen global health security, such as our leading contribution to combating the Ebola outbreak in West Africa. We will increase our investment, making greater use of the UK's world-leading expertise in public health and medical research.

5.137 We have led the global fight against Antimicrobial Resistance. In March 2015 we announced the new £195 million Fleming Fund to strengthen surveillance of drug resistance and laboratory capacity in developing countries. We will implement the UK AMR Strategy 2013–18 and deliver the new AMR Innovation Fund launched with China, bringing in a broad range of international partners. We will lobby for further international financing for research and innovation to tackle AMR over this Parliament.

5.138 We have established a £20 million UK Vaccines Network to bring together the best expertise from academia, philanthropic organisations and industry for developing and trialling new vaccines for infectious diseases. We will invest further in the UK Vaccines Network up to 2020.

5.139 We will also invest in new, large-scale research and development to combat the world's deadliest diseases. These include diseases with epidemic potential and those which affect the lives and livelihoods of millions in developing countries, building on the UK's major commitment to tackle malaria and neglected tropical diseases over the last Parliament.

5.140 **We will establish a new rapid response team of technical experts to deploy to help countries to investigate and control disease outbreaks.** This team will include epidemiologists, infection control specialists and researchers and will be on permanent standby. **We will expand our Emergency Medical Team to provide medical assistance to help contain outbreaks when needed**, including hundreds of doctors, nurses and specialist public health experts with field training.

Supporting global action to build stability and resilience

5.141 Global risks and rising instability require a stronger international response. We will strengthen our partnerships on building stability overseas with allies, the private sector and civil society organisations. We will work more with and through international organisations, including UN missions and agencies, the EU, NATO, which provides security support and capacity building, regional organisations such as the AU and the IFIs, which provide large-scale finance and technical expertise.

5.142 The UK helped to secure agreement in 2015 on the Global Goals for sustainable development, which set new momentum for improving global stability by bringing together goals to end extreme poverty with work on peace, economic growth, good governance, equality, human development, environmental sustainability and tackling climate change. We will press for their effective international implementation and lead the way in delivering them.

Chapter 6 – Promote Our Prosperity

Overview

6.1   National Security Objective 3 is to **promote our prosperity** – seizing opportunities, harnessing innovation to strengthen our national security, and working with industry to ensure we have the capabilities and equipment that we need. Our economic and national security go hand-in-hand. Our strong economy provides the foundation to invest in our security and global influence, which in turn provides more opportunities at home and overseas for us to increase our prosperity. A growing global economy helps to reduce poverty and build security for all.

6.2   This chapter sets out how the Government will **promote our economic security and opportunities globally**, including by championing global economic reform and strengthening our relationships with emerging economies. We will increase **innovation** and strengthen its contribution to our national security. We will work with the UK's **defence and security industries** and support their growth through exports and investment in skills.

A. Economic security and opportunity

6.3   We will continue to build on the secure and productive foundations of fiscal responsibility and investment.

6.4   Since 2010, the Government has pursued a long-term economic plan and taken difficult decisions to halve the deficit as a share of GDP. We have one of the fastest growing developed economies, with GDP now 6.4% above its pre-crisis peak in 2008. Employment has risen by 2.1 million since the start of the last Parliament. Wages are rising above inflation.

6.5   The Government is also boosting our long-term productivity to secure rising living standards. Our Productivity Plan aims to encourage long-term investment and promote a dynamic economy. The Fiscal Charter will require all future governments to maintain a budget surplus in normal times, ensuring the long-term economic security the UK needs.

6.6   Employment is at record levels. The Government is committed to building on this success and has set out its ambition to have the highest employment rate in the G7. We will give businesses the confidence to create more jobs over the next five years by continuing to get our public finances in order; investing in infrastructure; using our tax system to incentivise and not inhibit investment; and transforming education and training.

6.7   Our strong economy provides the foundation to invest in our security and enables us to project our influence across the world. It has enabled us to choose to invest 2% of GDP on defence and 0.7% of GNI on Official Development Assistance. We are the only major country to meet both these targets.

6.8   Our investment in national security ensures that we can provide a stable, secure country where people are able to do business, and in which others want to invest. Chapters 4 and 5 set out how we will ensure that our economy and businesses are resilient to shocks at home and abroad, and protected against threats such as serious and organised crime.

6.9   Overseas, we promote open and growing markets, advocate the rules-based international order and work to make multilateral institutions more effective.

Promoting prosperity overseas

6.10   As an open economy in an increasingly interconnected world, we need strong and sustainable global growth. Increased prosperity abroad can be expected to boost exports and improve the returns on our investments abroad. This benefits the UK, contributing to our economic stability and growth.

6.11   The global economy has continued to grow in the last five years, with millions of people lifted out of extreme poverty. Economic development overseas benefits the UK. Rising income is associated with reduced risk of conflict. This means that actions that support global prosperity lead to both direct and indirect benefits for the UK.

6.12   We will increase our efforts to build mutually beneficial, long-term, sustainable relationships with developing and emerging economies. We will support reforms in developing economies which will stimulate economic growth. We are also investing in climate change reduction and resilience programmes and there are significant trade and economic opportunities in helping drive low carbon transition across the globe; the current market is worth around £4 trillion and is growing at 4–5% a year.

6.13   To support growth and sustainable economic development in many of the poorest developing countries, we have already scaled up DFID's investment in economic development to almost 30% of bilateral programmes. We will use this money to unlock private and public investment in energy, infrastructure and urban development, creating jobs and reducing poverty. We will also double DFID's spending on improving tax systems and on tackling tax evasion and avoidance, and will put anti-corruption at the heart of our development relationships.

6.14   Emerging markets are an increasingly important economic presence. Between 1990 and 2000, they contributed 18% of global growth, compared with 82% for the advanced economies. But by 2020, growing markets are forecast to contribute 57% of world GDP growth, while advanced economies will contribute 43%. We will do more in emerging markets and in middle-income countries to encourage global economic growth. **We are creating a Prosperity Fund of £1.3 billion over the next five years** to promote the economic reform and development needed for growth in partner countries. Our priorities will include improving the business climate, competitiveness and operation of markets, energy and financial sector reform, and increasing the ability of partner governments to tackle corruption. As well as contributing to a reduction in poverty in recipient countries, we expect these reforms to create opportunities for international business, including UK companies.

6.15   Our established trading and investment partnerships with the world's most advanced economies will continue to be vitally important in driving global growth and UK prosperity. In 2014, we exported more manufactured goods to the US than to any other country and 50% of our exports were to Europe. The value of the UK's foreign direct investment stock increased by more than 9% during 2014, passing the £1 trillion level for the first time. The US and Europe remain the largest investors in the UK when measured by the value of foreign direct investment stock.

Global economic reform

6.16   In Chapter 5 we set out the work we are already doing to help ensure that global economic institutions are strengthened and their role in supporting development in fragile states is expanded. We will work through these institutions to build consensus on tackling global economic challenges.

6.17   We have led work through the G20 and OECD to tackle tax avoidance by international companies. Together with action that we have taken to address multinational tax avoidance in the UK, this is expected to raise around £1.6 billion in tax for the UK over the next five years. Through the IMF and the Financial Stability Board we are working to create more robust international frameworks for economic surveillance, financial regulation and standards, and crisis resolution.

6.18   The UK was the first major Western country to apply to join the new Asian Infrastructure Investment Bank. This is an opportunity to build stronger links with Asian countries from China to Indonesia. By being at the table from the start, we have shaped the Bank, which is now committed to the highest international standards. It will support economic growth in Asia and beyond, as well as create opportunities for UK business.

6.19   Trade liberalisation significantly boosts economic growth and contributes to global security. We will work to improve access to international markets, multilaterally through the World Trade Organization, through preferential trade deals with developing countries, and through EU negotiations with trading partners such as Japan and the US. We are seeking the conclusion and implementation of a comprehensive EU-US free trade agreement.

6.20   We will seek to create a level playing field for British firms, whose standards of corporate governance are among the highest in the world. We will work to eliminate tariff and non-tariff barriers, tackling corruption, developing British standards and regulations in international markets, and protecting intellectual property rights.

Emerging markets

6.21   We will invest in deepening our relationships with emerging economies as they take on increasing importance on the global stage. We will use our influence to build open markets, and encourage new powers to engage with the rules-based international order. For the largest economies we will strengthen our ties across the full range of government business, and develop our economic relationship through high-level Economic and Financial Dialogues.

6.22   Our engagement with China in recent years, following this model, has led to direct financial benefits for the UK – and reflects our ambition for the UK to be China's leading partner in the West. The UK is now one of the most popular destinations for Chinese investment in Europe. Our goods and services exports to China increased by 84% between 2010 and 2014, and up to £40 billion of trade and investment agreements were reached at the China State Visit in October 2015 alone. But engaging in this way also reflects a much wider goal to work more closely on the global stage with the economies of the future, supporting global and UK prosperity.

6.23   India presents burgeoning opportunities for British businesses. It is set to be the fastest growing major economy in 2015 and 2016, and by 2030 is projected to become the world's third biggest economy after the US and China. We are in a strong position to develop the UK-India trade relationship – we are the biggest G20 investor in India, and we have strong cultural links through the Commonwealth and the 1.5 million British Indians who live in the UK. We are strengthening our already strong economic partnership, including through the role of the City of London in raising finance for India's transformation, and through trade and investment. British and Indian companies announced new collaborations in November 2015, together worth more than £9 billion.

6.24   As the largest economy in Latin America, Brazil is increasingly an important partner for the UK. We have chosen to strengthen our economic relationship with Brazil through an Economic and Financial Dialogue, with the inaugural meeting in October 2015 paving the way for closer cooperation on infrastructure and financial services.

6.25   We will build on our close relationships with China, India and Brazil through the Economic and Financial Dialogues process. We will use a range of regular bilateral dialogues to strengthen our relationships with these and other key partners, building on a strong foundation of economic and commercial diplomacy. For example, Joint Economic and Trade Committees promote free trade and open markets with a wider group of countries, such as Mexico, Turkey, Vietnam and the Republic of Korea. The recent dialogue with Mexico led to agreements on financial services, audio-visual production, intellectual property and energy and telecoms regulation.

6.26   We will continue to take a strategic approach to our engagement with partners, and will go further in making this a cross-government effort. We will develop cross-government strategies, overseen by the NSC, which will bring together the Government's prosperity and security objectives for a set of priority countries, to promote global prosperity and support the UK's national interest. Designated Ministers will lead on developing high-level relationships, supported by a whole-of-government approach in the UK. Overseas, we will use our diplomatic network to provide the political access, relationships and economic advice which British business needs.

Open for business

6.27   As one of the most open economies in the world, with significant trade and financial links with other countries, we are the leading champion within the EU of open markets. Through the EU, we have free trade agreements covering more than 50 of our trading partners, which remove barriers to business and open up markets.

6.28   To maximise the opportunities from global prosperity, UK companies need to be ready to export and invest overseas – across emerging markets and with our traditional partners. The UK was the second largest exporter of services in 2014. In our drive for exports, we will support British businesses across all sectors to increase their exports and investment. Section C of this chapter sets out how we will work with the defence and security industries to increase their exports. We will use our diplomatic network to create access and opportunities for UK business.

6.29   Thriving and sustainable inward investment is central to our prosperity, supporting major investment in infrastructure, and improvements in the UK's productivity. Inward investment to the UK is £1.4 trillion, making us the second largest recipient of inward investment globally, and the largest in the EU. We will present a strong and consistent message to partners that the UK is open for business. Foreign investment is crucial for our prosperity and the UK welcomes it. There are no sectors in the UK closed to inward investment. Where any national security concerns may arise, the Government will quickly assess the risks and mitigation to provide greater certainty for investors.

Our secure and resilient trading environment

6.30   Together with our allies, our Diplomatic Service and our Armed Forces contribute to global stability and help secure the trade routes vital to our economy – for example, working with partners to counter piracy. This supports global prosperity and poverty reduction, and makes it easier and safer for British businesses to operate and trade overseas.

6.31   At home, our secure trading environment and our internationally recognised legal and financial system have enabled the UK to be a world leader in financial services. London is the world's premier international financial centre. Our intent is for the UK to remain the top choice for European and global bank headquarters.

6.32   As well as building resilience to financial crises, HM Treasury works with the Bank of England, the Financial Conduct Authority and international financial bodies to strengthen the resilience of the UK's finance sector to operational threats, including cyber crime. This work ensures that the UK's finance sector is one of the most stable, and is fully prepared to mitigate the impact of any risks.

6.33   The private sector holds critical information, data, intelligence, expertise, assets and resources. UK-based companies invest large sums in their own security, and the Government will continue to encourage, advise and support them to do this.

6.34   We will seek to develop long-term partnerships with industry built on trust and collaboration, through better sharing of information and expertise, and by encouraging industry to play a leading role. The Government will avoid regulation wherever possible.

B. Innovation

6.35   Innovation – generating ideas and putting them into practice to overcome challenges and exploit opportunities – drives the UK's economic strength, productivity and competitiveness. Innovation and our exploitation of science and technology are also vital to our national security. They underpin the equipment, capabilities and skills that give us an advantage over adversaries, and enable us to deal with threats and hazards now and in the future.

6.36   The global landscape for technological innovation has shifted. The private sector, not governments, drives today's rapid pace of technological change. In 2014, the top 20 global companies' research and development budgets alone amounted to over £100 billion. The UK conducts world-class innovation across all the major commercial technology sectors with national security applications, including aerospace, biotechnology and medical sciences, big data, cyber security, satellites, robotics and advanced materials.

6.37   We seek to work further with the private sector to make both government innovation and private sector contributions to national security more effective.

6.38   We have championed new approaches to innovation, through the Small Business Research Initiative, which has let more than £270 million of contracts, and by establishing a network of nine catapult centres across the UK to promote research and development collaboration between scientists, engineers and business and to help drive future economic growth.

6.39   We have increased our collaboration with industry, setting up the Defence, Cyber, and Security and Resilience Growth Partnerships to support the competitiveness and export success of defence and security products and services. As part of the Defence Growth Partnership, we are exploring different forms of financing to unlock greater private sector investment in defence innovation. The Government and industry have jointly funded the new Defence Solution Centre and the Security Innovation Demonstration Centre, which create new collaborative and commercially aware approaches to defence and security challenges.

6.40   The Government has invested in new technologies that have the potential to disrupt our adversaries. This includes cutting-edge research through the MOD's Defence Science and Technology Laboratory and the Home Office's Centre for Applied Science and Technology, working closely with industry and academia.

6.41   To secure operational advantage and control our costs into the future, we need to recognise and respond quickly to transformative ideas and technologies. These will come from outside the traditional national security field, as well as from our allies and in response to our adversaries. So we must find, listen to and work effectively with new partners. We must test unconventional ideas rigorously against traditional ones, and be prepared to take risks. And we must implement our new ideas before our adversaries do. In common with other countries facing similar challenges, we do not have all the answers, but continuing with our traditional mindset will not work.

6.42   **We will launch a defence innovation initiative** setting out the approach the MOD will take in more detail. Other departments will also incorporate these principles into their plans. Among other things, we will incentivise and remove obstacles to innovation, and foster a culture of innovation that takes a different approach to risk, investment planning and project management. The Government will strengthen departmental leadership on innovation and use Departmental Boards more effectively to drive progress on our innovation goals during this Parliament.

6.43   We will work with the UK's universities, start-up companies and small and medium-sized enterprises (SMEs), making creative thinking, science and technology central to our national security thinking. We will improve our technology scouting for new threats and opportunities, drawing in ideas and solutions pioneered in fields beyond defence and security. **We will create a new, cross-government Emerging Technology and Innovation Analysis Cell**, with close links to the private sector and academia to ensure that we identify these opportunities.

6.44   We will dedicate 1.2% of our defence budget to science and technology over this Parliament and, as part of the new £165 million Defence and Cyber Innovation Fund, increase funding to support the procurement of innovative solutions to the challenges facing the Armed Forces.

6.45   The Government will review which technologies we need to develop ourselves, and which we should obtain commercially and through partnership and joint investment with allies, academia and industry. We will maximise the scope for commercialisation of technologies developed for government national security purposes, encouraging economic growth and competitiveness, and explain the problems we need to solve rather than specifying in detail what the answers must look like. **We will establish a defence and security accelerator for government to help the private sector, allies and academia turn ideas into innovative equipment and services faster for national security users.** It will allow us to identify the best routes to develop specialist, sovereign capabilities, and those products with broader commercial and export potential. This will work closely with the Defence and the Security and Resilience Growth Partnerships.

6.46   Cyber security contributes £17 billion each year to the UK's economy. **We will encourage the creation and growth of a vibrant cyber security sector, including launching two innovation centres; supporting the best up-and-coming cyber SMEs; and helping to commercialise research in universities.**

6.47   As part of our focus on skills and increased interchange with the private sector and academia, **we will develop initiatives for the MOD workforce, including apprenticeships, focused on science, technology, engineering and maths and entrepreneurial skills.** We will provide our employees with opportunities to create their own start-ups, and make it easier to move between government, academia, private sector and in other countries.

6.48   We will work closely with, learn from and invest in joint research programmes with our allies and partners, many of whom are pursuing similar innovation initiatives. The US are pursuing their Third Offset Strategy, which aims to retain their military advantage into the future, and France has important technology programmes, especially in aerospace, maritime and space capabilities. We will also build on our important security relationships with partners such as Japan, and with multilateral forums, including NATO.

C. The defence and security industries and skills

6.49   The defence and security industries manufacture and support the equipment that our Armed Forces, law enforcement, security and intelligence agencies and our allies and partners use, and make a major contribution to our prosperity. In the UK they employ over 215,000 people, predominantly highly skilled, and support a further 150,000, as well as 6,500 apprentices. In 2014, both industries had a collective turnover of over £30 billion, including defence and security export orders worth £11.9 billion. Half of all firms in the sector expect to grow by at least 10% over the next year. The security sector, in particular, has grown on average five times faster than the rest of the UK economy since 2008.

6.50   We are one of the largest customers of defence and security products and services in the world. We will always strive to get the best value for money for the taxpayer and we will do so in a way that strengthens our economy and bolsters the long-term prosperity of people across the country. The Government remains committed to the principles set out in the 2012 White Paper *National Security Through Technology*. **We will refresh our defence industrial policy and take further action to help the UK's defence and security industries to grow and compete successfully.** We will drive greater innovation into our defence procurement, and ensure that future investment decisions contribute to a more dynamic and productive economy.

A more open, competitive and innovative sector

6.51   Over the next 10 years, we will spend £178 billion on defence equipment and equipment support. As a result of the Government's programme of defence transformation, the MOD is better able to deliver projects to time and cost. We have made significant improvements over the past five years but there is more to do. This relies on industry improving its performance as well as government.

6.52   We have carried out reforms to create more efficiency and greater transparency on costs. The 2013 White Paper *Better Defence Acquisition* and the subsequent Defence Reform Act 2014 have significantly changed the way the MOD undertakes single source, non-competitive procurement with the establishment of the Single Source Regulations Office (SSRO) as an independent regulator.

6.53   The Successor submarine and Type 26 Global Combat Ship programmes will be the first major projects delivered through single-source contracts overseen by the SSRO. As large national projects, they will also provide opportunities for new suppliers, including SMEs, to form part of the supply chain. We will work with our prime contractors to maximise these opportunities, including through the use of competition.

6.54   The UK operates one of the most open and competitive defence markets of any major country. We will continue to buy off-the-shelf products or services where they allow us to secure the necessary freedom of action and operational advantage. Exceptions will include:

- Highly classified or sensitive technologies, or those governed by export control or treaty restrictions.

- Capabilities necessary to maintain interoperability with important allies, but which they cannot or will not provide to the standard required by our Armed Forces.

- Capabilities where there is strategic, military and economic benefit for the UK from long-term collaboration with other nations.

6.55   **We will publish a new national shipbuilding strategy in 2016**, which will lay the foundations for a modern and efficient sector capable of meeting the country's future defence and security needs. The acquisition of the Type 26 Global Combat Ship will be crucial to the future of the UK's warship-building industry and form a central part of the strategy. We intend to start the manufacturing phase for the first ships once we have further matured the design. We will compete elements of the manufacturing work so that the programme delivers on time and to cost. As part of this plan, we will build a further two Offshore Patrol Vessels, providing continuity of shipbuilding work and additional capability for the Royal Navy in the short term. We will maintain our fleet of 19 frigates and destroyers. We will launch a concept study and then design and build a new class of lighter, flexible, exportable general purpose frigate to complement the Type 26 so that by the 2030s we can further increase the total number of frigates and destroyers.

6.56   We will continue to welcome inward investment and new entrants into the defence and security sector. We will benefit from the creativity and dynamism of the growing UK technology sector, and SMEs which might previously have gone overseas to exploit their ideas.

6.57   We will maximise the commercial opportunities for supplier companies arising from our national security procurements, and make these opportunities available to a broader range of potential suppliers.

6.58   It is important that industry's supply chains are robust, especially where they relate to sensitive components or services that cannot be procured from overseas. The MOD will adopt a more vigilant and systematic approach in certain sectors, such as those supporting the nuclear deterrent and high-grade cryptography, where this applies.

6.59   We will take action to enable SMEs and non-traditional suppliers to bid for defence and security contracts more easily. Building on the existing Defence Suppliers Forum, we have established dedicated forums to focus on the needs of small and medium-sized suppliers to ensure that we understand their concerns and priorities, and can maximise their contribution to our national security. In addition to the measures set out in the preceding section on innovation, we will:

- Develop the Defence, and Security and Resilience Growth Partnerships to make it easier for international partners to access all that British industry has to offer, ensuring that we are the preferred international partner for defence collaboration and innovation.

- Improve the transparency of future requirements in the security sector, and enable SMEs to partner with each other in bidding for government contracts that would be too big or complex for them to manage alone.

- Continue to simplify procurement processes, making them shorter and more open to innovative solutions so that more companies are able to compete more easily.

- Appoint a senior official in the MOD with responsibility for reducing the barriers faced by SMEs, increasing outreach and consultation.

6.60   As part of being international by design, we will participate in future international collaborative programmes in both the defence and security sectors where we have the right technology, skills and industrial capabilities, and where we can reduce our costs and share technology to mutual benefit, strengthening our defence relationships.

Enhancing support to exports and creating the best conditions for industry

6.61   Responsible defence and security exports, including equipment, services, sub-systems and through-life support, are essential for our security and prosperity. They directly sustain tens of thousands of jobs across the UK and generate economies of scale that reduce the cost of equipment to the Government and taxpayer. They underpin long-term relationships with our partners' national security organisations, and help us deliver wider foreign policy objectives.

6.62   The UK is a high-value economy, with high-end engineering, design and technology skills. We will focus on our national strengths, increasing government support to make business easier for both British industry and their international customers. We expect a similar level of commitment and cooperation from industry partners. We remain committed to operating our robust export licensing process to ensure that our defence and security exports accord with our values. **We will further enhance our support to the defence and security export sector**, and will:

- Establish a team in UKTI dedicated to supporting the negotiation and delivery of government-to-government deals by departments. These deals offer customers simplicity, reliability, access to our skills and advice, and a wider relationship with the UK. They are increasingly in demand from our partners.

- Make support for exports a core task for the MOD, with responsibility for managing all strategic defence export campaigns, overseen by the Defence Secretary and a new senior official post. This will create additional capacity to support these campaigns, including the training of international customers. We will adopt a more flexible approach to charging potential customers when supporting export campaigns where this is in our national interest. UKTI Defence and Security Organisation will continue to work with the sector to promote exports to potential customers.

• Ensure that future export potential is factored into our own equipment procurement decisions from the outset, and that potential customers are routinely invited to trials of British-developed military and security equipment.

• Prioritise government resources on those campaigns where it can make the most difference, and where industry is willing to invest its own resources.

Investing in skills and people

6.63   Our national security relies on the commitment and skills of people across the public and private sectors. We will continue to work with universities and the private sector so that we can recruit and retain national security experts with the right skills. In many areas, such as nuclear and cyber, we need specialists with high levels of technical expertise.

6.64   We start from a strong position, with a world-leading higher education system and strong and growing apprenticeship schemes. We encourage young people to study engineering and science as well as to develop leadership skills, including through the 3,300 Armed Forces cadet units across the UK which give over 130,000 young people the opportunity to develop personal skills and gain vocational qualifications. **We will spend £50 million to increase the number of cadet units in schools, bringing the total across the UK to 500 by 2020.**

6.65   The national security community is a leading provider of apprenticeships – the MOD and the Armed Forces are the largest providers of apprenticeships in the country. We continue to work closely with the private sector to invest in well-funded, high-quality apprenticeships that will supply them with the skilled workforce they require, including through the proposed new apprenticeship levy. **We will train at least 50,000 apprentices in defence between now and 2020.** We have worked with industry to create a new defence apprenticeship Trailblazer which, from 2016, will deliver a new systems engineering Masters apprenticeship programme, attracting new engineers into advanced systems engineering as well as up-skilling existing engineers.

6.66   Our nuclear deterrent relies on a skilled and capable workforce across the Royal Navy, the MOD and our suppliers. The UK's defence and civil nuclear programmes are both growing, requiring a collaborative approach to meeting the skills. The Government published *Sustaining Our Nuclear Skills* in partnership with industry this year, setting out a collaborative action plan. This includes creating a common skills framework for jobs in the public sector, developing cross-sector nuclear career paths and enhancing the way that nuclear careers are managed, to improve the retention of key skills.

6.67   Since 2011, our National Cyber Security Programme has invested in establishing training providers and a network of cyber education specialists. **We will speed this up, providing targeted training for those who wish to pursue careers in cyber security.** We will create a schools programme to identify and encourage talent among 14–17-year-olds across the UK, and new cyber security apprenticeships focused on particular sectors. We will scale up existing successful programmes, including the Cyber Security Challenge and GCHQ's 'Cyber First' undergraduate sponsorship scheme. We will also run a £20 million competition to open a new Institute of Coding, which will develop digital and computer science skills in the UK. Together these measures will ensure we have the professionals with the right cyber skills in the public and private sector that we require to remain a world leader in cyber security.

Chapter 7 – Implementation and Reform

Implementation and reform

7.1   This chapter sets out how we will implement this strategy over the next five years, including through changes to our national security structures. The Prime Minister will oversee progress on implementation through the NSC, supported by the National Security Adviser.

7.2   To support the NSC, **we will establish a new NSC committee to oversee implementation of this strategy. The Chancellor of the Duchy of Lancaster will chair it.**

7.3   Individual departments and their Ministers will have responsibility for implementing commitments that they own. The implementation structure is set out below. The Cabinet Office will produce an annual update to Parliament on progress in delivering our commitments.

7.4   As part of the implementation phase, government departments will conduct impact assessments to determine effects of decisions made pursuant to the National Security Strategy and Strategic Defence and Security Review, where these are required in particular in relation to safety, the environment, sustainable development and equality and diversity.

7.5   In developing this strategy, we sought the views of external experts, our allies and the public. We have spoken to over 50 different organisations including academia, think tanks, non-governmental organisations and industry throughout the UK. We have discussed our analysis and approach with our closest allies, including in NATO and the EU. We received around 2,000 contributions from members of the public. We are extremely grateful to all of those who contributed their expertise.

7.6   We have ensured that this strategy is fully aligned with available resources. All government departments are expected to meet high levels of efficiency. Alongside the development of the strategy, we have scrutinised the efficiency of national security spend. The Cabinet Secretary led a process which has identified more than £11 billion of savings from MOD, the security and intelligence agencies and cross-government counter-terrorism spending. We are re-investing these savings in our national security priorities.

Government structures

7.7   To deliver this strategy we will enhance our national security structures which will promote our further integrated, whole-of-government approach.

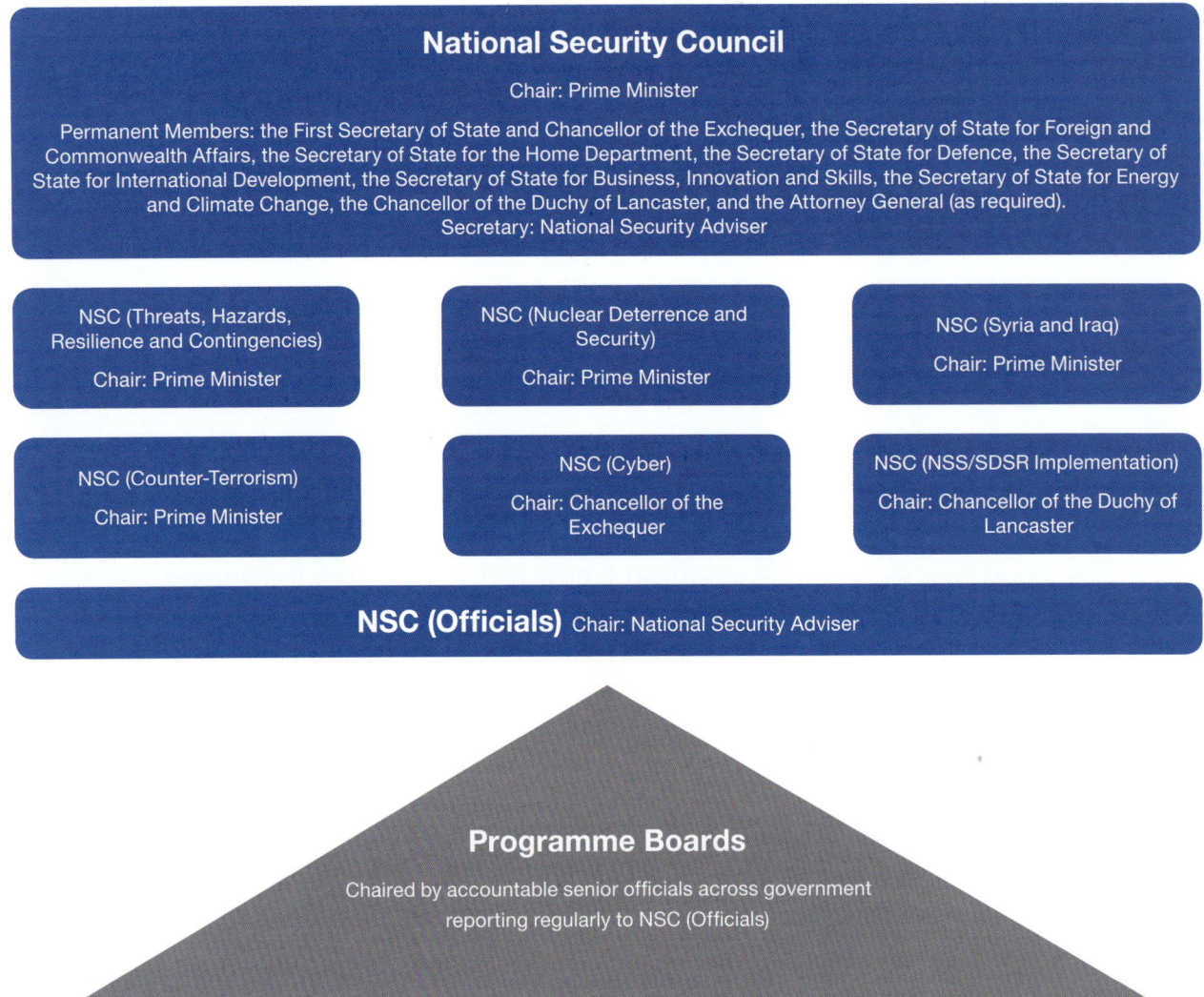

Crisis response

7.8   The Government needs to deal with crises that emerge rapidly, and multiple crises at the same time. We have a strong record of dealing with such situations, but continue to seek to shorten response times.

7.9   In 2010 we established the NSC to provide collective strategic leadership on national security and crisis situations. The National Security Adviser coordinates the work of the NSC, and provides policy advice through the National Security Secretariat. The Joint Intelligence Committee, led by its Chairman, provides strategic intelligence assessment. They also ensure that Ministers and senior officials receive the advice and analysis they need in the Cabinet Office Briefing Rooms (COBR), which acts as the national crisis response mechanism and the operational arm of the NSC during a crisis.

7.10   Five years on from establishing these structures, **we will launch a review of how we support the NSC and COBR during crises**. This will identify how we provide all the support and information that Ministers require in a challenging threat environment. The end result will be a resilient and agile structure, able to deal with a wider range of threats and hazards in the 21st century and to plug into local, national and international partners. As part of this, we will upgrade our crisis response infrastructure, including COBR and Departmental capabilities.

Early warning, horizon scanning and use of open source data

7.11   We have already established new early warning processes on countries at risk of instability, and extended our established domestic early warning process for hazards to cover international incidents. We have brought together experts to horizon scan opportunity and risk. We have enhanced intelligence analysis skills across government, including through professional development.

7.12   The large volume of information available now – ranging from 'Big Data', vast open source resources, diplomatic and military reporting, to secret intelligence – provides an opportunity for greater understanding. But the complexity and volume of the data involved, either through sheer size or speed of collection, makes analysing it with conventional techniques more difficult.

7.13   The UK has a strong reputation globally in data analytics. The Alan Turing Institute, headquartered at the British Library, will be a world-class facility to tackle the most challenging Big Data problems, forming a partnership of industry, government and academia.

7.14   In government, we will ensure that early warning, horizon scanning programmes, open source material and data analytics shape policy development. We have taken steps to ensure that horizon scanning across government focuses on strategic priorities, draws on the best expertise available and feeds effectively into policy development. We will go further to join up horizon scanning between national security and other policy areas to enable a rigorous assessment of emerging challenges and opportunities.

7.15   **We will review the structure for strategic assessment within central government.** This will also consider how we equip and train our analysts, promote challenge within government thinking and share threat information.

Joint Units

7.16   We are creating a number of new, issue-focused cross-government teams to remove duplication, consolidate national security expertise and make the most efficient use of it across government.

7.17   These will follow the precedent of existing high-performing cross-government teams such as the Stabilisation Unit and the International Energy Unit. **We will establish new policy-making and delivery Joint Units in 2016:**

- A **Euro-Atlantic Security Policy Unit**, hosted by the FCO, which will bring together diplomatic and defence expertise to develop and implement UK policy for NATO and for EU Common Security and Defence Policy; provide strategic direction to our Brussels delegations; and provide national representation to NATO and relevant EU committees.

- A joint unit for **International Counter-Terrorism Strategy**, hosted by the Home Office, consolidating existing expertise within the Home Office and FCO.

- An **Arms Control and Counter-Proliferation Centre**, hosted by the MOD, which will consolidate in a single location the expertise and policy-making currently in the MOD, FCO, and Department of Energy and Climate Change.

- An **Exports Controls Unit**, hosted by BIS, to provide coordinated cross-government operation of export controls.

- A **Gulf Strategy Unit**, hosted by the Cabinet Office, to coordinate UK engagement with the Gulf in order to deliver the NSC's long-term strategy and maximise benefits to the UK.

- A **UN Peacekeeping Unit**, hosted by the FCO, consolidating existing MOD and FCO expertise to formulate UK policy on UN peacekeeping missions.

- We will also establish in 2016 a single provider of government **National Security Vetting Services**, based on the MOD model, to ensure we remain resilient against the insider threat.

7.18   We remain committed to ensuring that our defence and security workforce is as inclusive as possible. A diverse workforce, with varied backgrounds, perspectives and styles of thinking, is better able to tackle emerging crises and to produce innovative, challenging policy advice for Ministers. It will help us to improve the intelligence, law enforcement and defence understanding of, and relationships with broader communities. **We will establish a security and defence diversity network, sharing best practice and addressing our shared challenges, to drive development of a more diverse and inclusive national security community.**

7.19   Our ability to implement and deliver our vision is underpinned by the knowledge and skills of our people. We intend to take a more strategic shared approach across government, including by ensuring our education and training establishments work more closely together. These include the Diplomatic Academy, the Defence Academy, the Emergency Planning College and the College of Policing. **We will establish a virtual National Security Academy** which will act as a hub for these organisations to share, develop and maintain critical knowledge and skills across the national security community, leading to greater coherence and common professional standards.

7.20   We will regularly review the effectiveness of these new structures and create further joint units where they will deliver benefits.

Annex A – Summary of the National Security Risk Assessment 2015

National Security Risk Assessment 2015

1.   This is a summary of the National Security Risk Assessment (NSRA) 2015, which follows the original assessment in 2010 and a refresh in 2012. We will review the full NSRA on a regular basis.

2.   Against the context of developments and implications described in Chapter 3, the 2015 NSRA places the domestic and overseas risks we face into three tiers, according to judgement of **both likelihood and impact**. Tier One risks are the highest priority based on high likelihood and/or high impact. The 2015 assessment includes a greater number of Tier One and Tier Two risks than in 2012. This reflects both the impact of threats and hazards, and the development of risks since 2010.

3.   The NSRA is intended to inform strategic judgement, not forecast every risk. Many of the risks are interdependent, or could materialise at the same time. Our approach to risk management will need to take this into account.

The next five years

4.   The following are judged to be the Tier One risks over the next five years:

i.   **Terrorism:** This will remain the most direct and immediate threat to our domestic security and overseas interests. ISIL, Al Qa'ida and affiliates remain committed to attacking UK and Western targets.

ii. **Cyber:** The cyber threats to the UK are significant and varied. They include cyber terrorism, fraud and serious and organised crime, espionage, and disruption of CNI as it becomes more networked and dependent on technology, including networks and data held overseas. Cyber risks underpin many of the other risks we face.

iii. **International Military Conflict:** The risk is growing. Although it is unlikely that there will be a direct military threat to the UK itself, there is a greater possibility of international military crises drawing in the UK, including through our treaty obligations. Our ability to respond effectively will be made harder by the growing use of asymmetric and hybrid tactics by states, combining economic coercion, disinformation, proxies, terrorism and criminal activity, blurring the boundaries between civil disorder and military conflict.

iv. **Instability Overseas:** Since 2010 instability has spread significantly, especially in our extended neighbourhood, to the south in the Middle East and northern Africa and to the east in Ukraine.

v. **Public Health:** Disease, particularly pandemic influenza, emerging infectious diseases and growing Antimicrobial Resistance, threatens lives and causes disruption to public services and the economy. The UK's vulnerability is increased by our large population and open society.

vi. **Major Natural Hazards:** Events such as severe weather and major flooding can cost lives, cause disruption to Critical National Infrastructure and provision of essential services, and have a significant economic cost.

The longer term

5.   Over the longer term, the main drivers of the impact and likelihood of risk are changes in technology, and the geopolitical and global economic context. Climate change is increasingly a risk to the UK, with the full effects on UK national security more likely to be seen after 2035.

6.   The following aspects of the Tier One and Two risks may become even more likely and/or have a greater impact over the longer term:

- Antimicrobial Resistance.

- A range of cyber related threats.

- Chemical and biological attacks against the UK or its forces.

- Pressure on allies or undermining of our military and economic alliances and institutions.

- Emerging infectious diseases.

- Serious and organised crime, e.g. human trafficking.

- Proliferation: acquisition of nuclear, chemical and biological weapons, and advanced conventional weapons by state and non-state actors.

NSRA 2015 Priority Risks

7.   The NSC places the domestic and overseas risks we face into three tiers, **based on a judgement of the combination of both likelihood and impact**. This is not, therefore, a simple ranking of their importance.

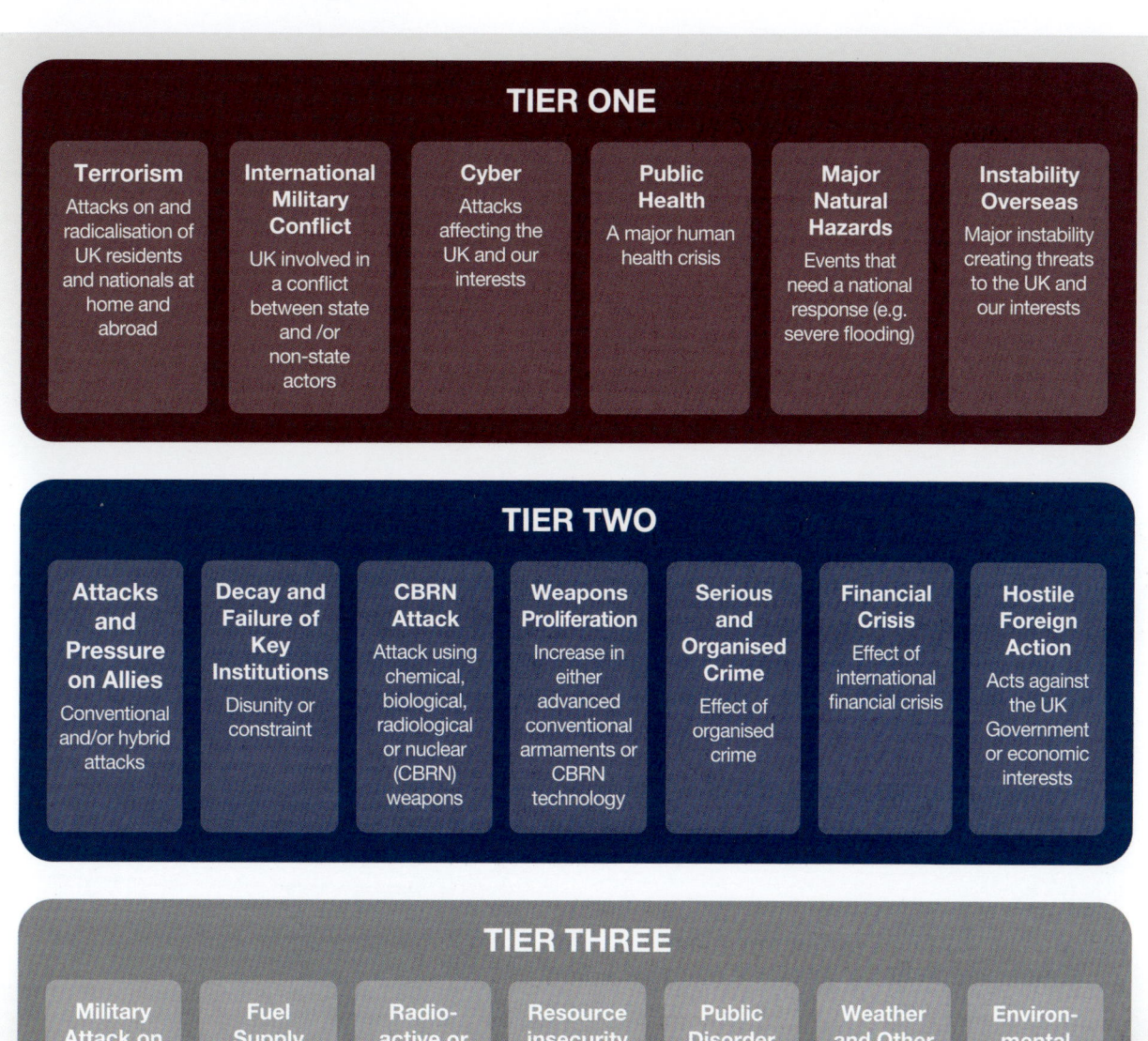

TIER ONE

Terrorism	**International Military Conflict**	**Cyber**	**Public Health**	**Major Natural Hazards**	**Instability Overseas**
Attacks on and radicalisation of UK residents and nationals at home and abroad	UK involved in a conflict between state and /or non-state actors	Attacks affecting the UK and our interests	A major human health crisis	Events that need a national response (e.g. severe flooding)	Major instability creating threats to the UK and our interests

TIER TWO

Attacks and Pressure on Allies	**Decay and Failure of Key Institutions**	**CBRN Attack**	**Weapons Proliferation**	**Serious and Organised Crime**	**Financial Crisis**	**Hostile Foreign Action**
Conventional and/or hybrid attacks	Disunity or constraint	Attack using chemical, biological, radiological or nuclear (CBRN) weapons	Increase in either advanced conventional armaments or CBRN technology	Effect of organised crime	Effect of international financial crisis	Acts against the UK Government or economic interests

TIER THREE

Military Attack on the UK, Overseas Territories or Bases	**Fuel Supply**	**Radio-active or Chemical Release**	**Resource insecurity**	**Public Disorder**	**Weather and Other Natural Hazards**	**Environ-mental Events**
	Disruption or price instability	Major malicious or accidental release	Disruption to international supplies (e.g. food, minerals)	Widespread public disorder	Such as severe heatwaves or cold weather	Such as animal diseases or severe air pollution

Annex B – Glossary

3 Commando Brigade	Very high readiness amphibious brigade, trained to operate both on land and at sea.
16 Air Assault Brigade	Very high readiness brigade, trained to operate by parachute, from helicopters and from aircraft.
A400M Atlas	Long-range, heavy-lift military transport aircraft.
Accelerator	A Government-backed service designed to help small and medium-sized businesses bring new ideas to market more quickly.
Africa Peace Facility	EU-funded mechanism to support peace and security in Africa, as part of the Africa-EU partnership.
Air Group	Large military aviation group comprising combat, transport and surveillance aircraft.
Air Policing Mission	Use of military aircraft in peacetime to preserve the integrity of a specified area of airspace.
Antimicrobial Resistance (AMR)	Resistance of micro-organisms which cause infection to a medicine that would normally kill them or stop their growth.
Apache	Attack helicopter.
Armed Forces Covenant	The relationship between the nation, the Government and the Armed Forces. Its principles are enshrined in law through the Armed Forces Act 2011.
Armoured Infantry Brigade	War-fighting brigade, comprising Challenger 2 tanks and Warrior infantry fighting vehicles, supported by artillery, engineer and logistic support elements.
Article 5	Article of the North Atlantic Treaty 1949, which states that an armed attack on one Ally shall be considered to be an attack on all Allies.
Association of South East Asian Nations	Political and economic organisation of South East Asian countries: Brunei; Burma; Cambodia; Indonesia; Laos; Malaysia; Philippines; Singapore; Thailand; and Vietnam.
Astute Class	Conventionally armed, nuclear-powered submarine.
AU	African Union; a union of 54 countries in Africa.

BBC World Service	A major international broadcasting service, part of the British Broadcasting Corporation.
BMD	Ballistic Missile Defence.
Border Force	Government organisation, responsible for immigration and customs controls for people and goods entering the UK.
Brimstone	Air-launched precision missile used against ground targets.
British Council	The UK's international organisation for cultural relations and educational opportunities.
C130J Hercules	Long-range, heavy-lift military transport aircraft.
C17	Long-range military transport aircraft for large or heavy loads.
Centre for Cyber Assessment	Provides independent, all-source cyber assessment for the Government.
CERT-UK	UK Computer Emergency Response Team, responsible for national cyber security incident management.
Chinook	Heavy-lift helicopter.
COBR	Cabinet Office Briefing Rooms, from where the Government's response to crises is coordinated.
Combined Joint Expeditionary Force	The UK-France combined reaction force of up to 10,000 personnel available to respond rapidly to crises.
Common Security and Defence Policy	An integral part of the EU's comprehensive approach towards crisis management, drawing on civilian and military resources.
Conflict, Stability and Security Fund	Government fund which brings together work on conflict, stability, security and peacekeeping in states where we have key interests.
Critical National Infrastructure (CNI)	Elements of national infrastructure which are critical to national security, defence or the functioning of the state.
Cyber First	Scheme to support talented undergraduates identified for a cyber security career.
Cyber Security Challenge	Competitions encouraging people to test their skills and to consider a career in cyber.
Dark web	Parts of the internet not normally accessible by the public or commercial internet search engines.
Defence Engagement	Ministry of Defence and Armed Forces non-combat activities with international partners which contribute to stability, security and prosperity.

DFID	Department for International Development; a UK Government department.
EU	European Union.
EU-Mercosur Trade Agreement	Free Trade Agreement between the EU, Argentina, Brazil, Paraguay, Uruguay and Venezuela.
F35 Lightning	Fifth generation multi-role combat aircraft.
FCO	Foreign and Commonwealth Office; a UK Government department.
Five Eyes	Australia, Canada, New Zealand, UK and US intelligence sharing community.
Five Power Defence Arrangements	Defence agreements between the UK, Australia, New Zealand, Malaysia and Singapore.
Fleming Fund	A UK Government fund to build a worldwide network of laboratories to monitor trends in drug-resistant infection in developing countries, and to tackle Antimicrobial Resistance.
G20	Group of 20 of the world's leading industrial nations.
G7	Group of 7 of the world's leading industrial nations: Canada, France, Germany, Italy, Japan, UK, US.
Galileo	European global navigation satellite system.
GCC	Gulf Cooperation Council, comprising Bahrain, Kuwait, Oman, Qatar, Saudi Arabia and the United Arab Emirates.
GCHQ	Government Communications Headquarters; the centre for the Government's signal intelligence activities.
GDP	Gross Domestic Product.
Global Goals	The 17 goals adopted at the United Nations General Assembly in September 2015 to end extreme poverty and ensure prosperity for all.
GNI	Gross National Income.
International Financial Institutions (IFI)	A generic term for financial institutions that operate on an international level and involve governments pooling resources to perform financial activities on behalf of them all.
International Monetary Fund (IMF)	Organisation of 188 countries working to foster global monetary cooperation, secure financial stability, facilitate international trade and reduce poverty around the world.
ISIL	The Islamic State of Iraq and the Levant – also known as Islamic State, Da'esh or Islamic State of Iraq and Syria (ISIS) – a terrorist organisation based in Iraq and Syria.

Joint Expeditionary Force	UK-led high readiness force for responding rapidly to crises, unilaterally or as part of a wider coalition, involving Denmark, Estonia, Latvia, Lithuania, the Netherlands and Norway.
Joint Force 2025	The UK's highly capable, expeditionary force that will be able to project power globally.
Joint Security Fund	New additional fund for the Armed Forces and the security and intelligence agencies.
Lancaster House Treaty	Defence and security cooperation treaty between the UK and France signed in 2010.
Landing Platform Dock	Amphibious assault command ship able to deploy and recover Royal Marines by helicopter and boat.
Landing Ship Dock	Amphibious assault support ship, equipped with a dock.
Maritime Patrol Aircraft	Long-range surveillance aircraft, primarily for anti-submarine warfare, with an overland capability.
Maritime Task Group	Large naval group comprising an aircraft carrier, amphibious ships, submarines, destroyers, frigates, mine counter-measure vessels, support ships and aircraft.
Merlin Mk 2	Anti-submarine variant of the Merlin medium-lift helicopter.
Merlin Mk 4	Commando variant of the Merlin medium-lift helicopter.
Missile Defence Centre	A UK Government and industry partnership for working with allies and partners on ballistic missile defence issues.
MOD	Ministry of Defence; a UK Government department.
National Maritime Information Centre	UK centre which coordinates maritime security information.
National Security Objectives	High-level, enduring and mutually supporting objectives that deliver our national security strategy.
NATO	North Atlantic Treaty Organization.
NCA	National Crime Agency; a non-Ministerial Government department.
NGO	Non-governmental organisation.
Northern Group	Group of 12 nations – Denmark, Estonia, Finland, Germany, Iceland, Latvia, Lithuania, the Netherlands, Norway, Poland, Sweden and the UK – formed to promote more effective defence and security cooperation in northern Europe.
NPT	Treaty on the Non-Proliferation of Nuclear Weapons 1970.

NSC	National Security Council; the main forum for collective discussion of the Government's objectives for national security and how best to deliver them.
NSRA	National Security Risk Assessment; a comparison and prioritisation of risks to UK national security interests.
NSS	National Security Strategy.
OECD	Organisation for Economic Cooperation and Development; an international organisation based in Paris.
Official Development Assistance (ODA)	Financial assistance for the economic development and welfare of developing countries.
OSCE	Organization for Security and Cooperation in Europe; an intergovernmental organisation based in Vienna.
Overseas Territories	The 14 territories that fall under UK jurisdiction but which are not part of the UK.
Protector	UK programme for future armed, remotely piloted surveillance aircraft.
Puma	Medium-lift battlefield helicopter.
Queen Elizabeth Class aircraft carrier	New class of aircraft carrier for the Royal Navy.
RAF	Royal Air Force.
Reaper	UK's current armed, remotely piloted surveillance aircraft.
Resolute Support Mission	NATO's ongoing mission in Afghanistan to provide further support to Afghan security forces and institutions.
Rivet Joint	Signals intelligence and surveillance aircraft.
Sentinel	Intelligence, surveillance and reconnaissance aircraft.
Sentry	Surveillance, command and control aircraft.
Shadow	Intelligence, surveillance and reconnaissance aircraft.
Skynet 5	Military communications satellite network.
Small Business Research Initiative	A group that promotes innovative ideas from industry to address public sector challenges.
SMEs	Small and medium-sized enterprises.
Sovereign Base Areas	UK's sovereign areas in Cyprus.
SSBN	Ship Submersible Ballistic Nuclear; a nuclear-armed, nuclear-powered submarine.

SSN	Ship Submersible Nuclear; a conventionally armed, nuclear-powered submarine.
SSRO	Single Source Regulations Office; an independent regulator of non-competitive defence contracts.
Stabilisation Unit	UK civil-military unit supporting Government efforts to tackle instability overseas.
Stormshadow	Long-range, air-launched precision missile for use against hardened targets.
Successor	Future nuclear-armed, nuclear-powered submarines.
Trident	Nuclear missile system in Vanguard Class submarines.
Type 23 Frigate	Multi-role warship designed primarily for anti-submarine warfare in service with the Royal Navy.
Type 26 Global Combat Ship	New Royal Navy multi-role warship to replace the current Type 23 frigates in their anti-submarine warfare role.
Type 45 Destroyer	Multi-role warship designed primarily for air defence in service with the Royal Navy.
Typhoon	Multi-role combat aircraft in service with the RAF.
UKTI	UK Trade and Investment; a Government department that works with UK-based businesses in international markets and supports overseas companies doing business in the UK.
UN	United Nations.
USAID	US Agency for International Development.
Vanguard Class	Current class of nuclear-armed, nuclear-powered submarines in service with the Royal Navy.
Very High Readiness Joint Task Force	NATO's new rapid reaction force.
Voluntary Sector Civil Protection Forum	Government forum for maximising the voluntary sector contribution to civil protection arrangements.
Voyager	Air-to-air refuelling and military transport aircraft.
Watchkeeper	Remotely piloted surveillance aircraft.
Wildcat	New light maritime and battlefield helicopter.